Serving Young Teens and 'Tweens

Recent titles in
Libraries Unlimited
Professional Guides for Young Adult Librarians

C. Allen Nichols and Mary Anne Nichols, Series Editors

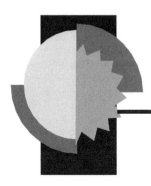

Serving Young
Teens and 'Tweens

Edited by
Sheila B. Anderson

Foreword by James M. Rosinia

Libraries Unlimited Professional Guides for Young Adult Librarians Series
C. Allen Nichols and Mary Anne Nichols, Series Editors

LIBRARIES
UNLIMITED
A Member of the Greenwood Publishing Group

Westport, Connecticut • London

Library of Congress Cataloging-in-Publication Data

Serving young teens and 'tweens / edited by Sheila B. Anderson ; foreword by James M. Rosinia.
    p. cm. — (Libraries Unlimited professional guides for young adult librarians series,
ISSN 1532–5571)
  Includes bibliographical references and index.
  ISBN 1–59158–259–8 (pbk. : alk. paper)
  1. Libraries and teenagers—United States. 2. Young adults' libraries—Activity programs—
United States. 3. Young adults' libraries—Collection development—United States.
4. Teenagers—Books and reading—United States. 5. Preteens—Books and reading—
United States. 6. Young adult literature—Bibliography. I. Anderson, Sheila B.
  Z718.5.S493   2007
  027.62'6—dc22   2006030666

British Library Cataloguing in Publication Data is available.

Library of Congress Catalog Card Number: 2006030666
ISBN: 1-59158-259-8
ISSN: 1532-5571

First published in 2007

Libraries Unlimited, 88 Post Road West, Westport, CT 06881
A Member of the Greenwood Publishing Group, Inc.
www.lu.com

Printed in the United States of America

The paper used in this book complies with the
Permanent Paper Standard issued by the National
Information Standards Organization (Z39.48–1984).

10 9 8 7 6 5 4 3 2 1

As a middle sibling,
I dedicate this book
to my older brother, Larry,
and to my younger brother, Brian,
for the role that they played
in shaping my life as a young teen.

Contents

Series Foreword

We firmly believe in young adult library services and advocate for teens whenever we can. We are proud of our association with Libraries Unlimited and Greenwood Publishing Group and grateful for their acknowledgment of the need for additional resources for teen-serving librarians. We intend for this series to fill those needs, providing useful and practical handbooks for library staff. Readers will find some theory and philosophical musings, but for the most part, this series will focus on real-life library issues with answers and suggestions for frontline librarians.

Our passion for young adult librarian services continues to reach new peaks. As we travel to present workshops on the various facets of working with teens in public libraries, we are encouraged by the desire of librarians everywhere to learn what they can do in their libraries to make teens welcome. This is a positive sign, since too often libraries choose to ignore this underserved group of patrons. We hope you find this series to be a useful tool in fostering your own enthusiasm for teens.

C. Allen Nichols
Mary Ann Nichols
Series Editors

Foreword

James M. Rosinia

"A class of sixth graders." What mental picture do these five words paint? Anyone who has had any experience with young adolescents ("y.a.'s") knows firsthand just how diverse young people between the ages of ten and fourteen can be. These years are marked by rapid and remarkable growth, which is most apparent in y.a.'s physical development. But equally dramatic changes are also taking place in their cognitive abilities and socioemotional lives. To further complicate things during this time of change, there is also great diversity—diversity within the individual (i.e., individuals do not develop physically, cognitively, and socioemotionally at the same time and at the same rate) and across the age cohort. This means that while it is normal for a twelve-year-old to begin to physically resemble an adult but still have the cognitive abilities and/or emotional maturity of a child, it is also normal for another twelve-year-old to have the cognitive abilities and/or emotional maturity approaching those of an adult but still physically resemble a child.

No two y.a.'s are alike in all respects. One size does not fit all. Fortunately, public librarians are in a position to serve each y.a. as an individual even as they purchase material and develop programs to serve the group. In meeting the varied needs of the communities they serve, public librarians are accustomed to developing a diverse collection of material and offering a wide range of programs that respond to those needs.

They may, for instance, develop a collection of Spanish-language material to respond to the linguistic needs of the community, or purchase more recorded books in response to requests by workers whose commutes have increased, or add large-print items to serve their aging population.

Simply by doing what they do best—by being responsive to the needs of those they serve when they develop collections and design programs—public librarians can do much to help y.a.'s. As with all school-age students, young adolescents need resources that will help them with assignments—resources that may not be available to them at home, such as subject-specific reference works or access to back issues of periodicals. They also have a wide range of leisure time interests, and, on what might seem like a daily basis, they develop passionate (if passing) interests in new things from magic to makeup, cartooning to crafts. They therefore appreciate access to information about their interests, whether from the collection or through programs.

Young adolescents also have many questions about the powerful changes and feelings they are experiencing, and they need easy access to accurate information that will normalize and explain these changes and feelings and will help them make a number of informed personal decisions. And, just as they want, and *need*, to test their new physical powers by exercising and stretching their developing muscles, they also want, and *need*, to stretch their developing cognitive powers by reading speculative genres such as science fiction and fantasy. Simply by developing collections and designing programs with their questions and interests in mind, librarians can do much to help y.a.'s develop into healthy adults.

But y.a.'s have other unique developmental needs. In what has been called the second process of separation-individuation (the first occurring in early childhood), y.a.'s are moving away from their immediate family and into a wider—and scarier—world. As they begin to develop a self, it is important that they encounter adults other than their parents. At a time of life when they are painfully self-conscious, it is important that these adults be nonjudgmental, supportive, and respectful. The public library has always prided itself on being a nonjudgmental and welcoming community institution. It is crucial that public librarians treat y.a.'s and their questions and requests with the same respect they would show to the parents or to the Chair of the Board of Trustees.

The world in which y.a.'s live today is very different than the world in which their parents grew up, but the developmental changes and needs remain the same. The parents of today's young adolescents spent hours on the telephone with their friends. Today's young adolescents spend hours e-mailing and instant messaging. While the technology has changed, the need to experiment with intimacy (albeit at a distance) is the same. And the y.a.'s of the future will experience the same developmental changes and will have the same unique needs.

By its mission, its place in the community, and the training and experience of its staff, the public library is uniquely positioned to make a significant contribution during what the Carnegie Council on Adolescent Development refers to as our "last best chance" to make a difference in the lives of young adolescents.

The Search Institute has identified forty "developmental assets" that have the power to influence the choices y.a.'s make during these critical years. Of these, twenty are "internal assets"—qualities and traits such as caring, honesty, restraint, sense of purpose. The remaining twenty are "external assets"—the positive experiences young people receive from the world around them, experiences that the adults in their lives are in a position to affect. There are many ways in which the staff of a public library can build assets: by offering supportive adult role models, by viewing youth as resources, by providing opportunities for y.a.'s to be of service to others, and, most importantly, by helping send the message that the community values youth.

When I was on the staff of the Center for Early Adolescence at the University of North Carolina at Chapel Hill, we worked with those who were in a position to develop programs and provide services for y.a.'s: middle school teachers, after-school program planners, youth ministers, pediatricians and nurses, parent educators, and librarians. The common theme of all our work was "developmental responsiveness." Since all of these professionals had experienced this time of life themselves, we reminded them of the unique characteristics and developmental needs of y.a.'s. We then suggested ways in which their programs and services could be designed to meet those needs.

Parents know that y.a.'s are always eating as their bodies sense the need for fuel to support their physical growth, and parents struggle to keep refrigerators and pantries stocked with a balance of the nutritionally bankrupt snacks their children like, as well as the healthier foods their growing bodies need. In the same way, the emotional and intellectual hunger of y.a.'s needs to be met.

Young adolescents have sharp appetites for speculative fiction that stretches their cognitive powers. They want to ingest information on a wide variety of topics—from physical development and interpersonal relationships to hobbies and sports. And they are ravenous for respect and starving for support.

By stocking the shelves with a diversity of material—the "snacks" they like, as well as the titles they need—and by thoughtfully planning programs, public librarians can do much to prepare a feast for them. By recognizing their individuality and by serving them with respect, public librarians can insure that y.a.'s feel invited to have a seat at the table.

Preface

Please. Today is the day to have your attention. Something has transpired across the nation. We don't have any information now. Trust us that we would tell you. Please act like the mature sixth graders that you are. You're not in elementary school anymore. —(Perlstein, Linda. *Not Much Just Chillin': The Hidden Lives of Middle Schoolers.* New York: Farrar, Straus and Giroux, 2003, p. 28.)

Shortly after I finished editing my first book, *Serving Older Teens* (Libraries Unlimited 2004), and writing my second book, *Extreme Teens: Library Services to Nontraditional Young Adults* (Libraries Unlimited 2005), I considered compiling another book. This time, I wanted to focus on young teens. This notion became solidified after two things happened in my life. First, I witnessed the transformation of my cousin, Rachel, as she rapidly progressed from a child to a teenager. As a teen advocate and a former young adult librarian, I thought that observing this transition would be easy. I soon realized, however, that it was difficult for me to accept the fact that she was no longer a child. When reading books published for teens that I would typically recommend to library patrons, I became more critical of books for my own family members. This experience helped me realize even more that 'tweens and young teens are a special breed, needing individualized attention.

My second inspiration for compiling this book came from reading and reviewing a book for the library journal *Voice of Youth Advocates*. At the time, I regularly volunteered to review books intended to help adults learn about teenagers. When *Not Much Just Chillin': The Hidden Lives of Middle Schoolers* showed up on my doorstep, I dug right in. I envied the author, a *Washington Post* education reporter, who spent a year studying teenagers at a suburban Maryland middle school and later wrote about their lives. Early in the book, the author focuses on the sudden changes that middle school students face when they leave elementary school. They are thrown into a new world, where the focus is suddenly on the social scene. Parents are especially baffled during this time, wondering why their child, who used to be sweet and loving, is suddenly moody and distant. They are developing at various rates, some quickly with acne and breasts, while others still resemble children with baby faces. In light of the insights I had gained, I decided that librarians might benefit from having a book about how to better serve this age group.

I was captivated by Perlstein's description of the students' reactions to the terrorist attacks on September 11, 2001, and how the school staff dealt with the situation. Like other Americans, I will never forget where I was on September 11, 2001. Also, like other Americans, my family and I were in the midst of a typical, calm day that turned into an unpredictable and catastrophic one. I was on my way to the grocery store with my mother in New Jersey when my younger brother called and told us to turn on the television. He had been washing dishes, listening to the Howard Stern show, when he learned about the terrorist attacks. A few hours after hearing the news, I reluctantly drove to work in Delaware, fearfully crossing a bridge while glued to the radio. Halfway there, I learned that Governor Minner had declared a state of emergency, and I returned to New Jersey, where I was saddened by what I saw on television for the rest of the day. Of course, an adult has a different perception of national events than children or teens. When I was in middle school, I remember being told that the *Challenger* had exploded, and we listened to the news over the school intercom. As an adult, I found it fascinating to read Chapter 2 in Perlstein's book, "Everyone Else Thinks It's a Stupid Plane Crash." At first, the middle school students were glad to be getting out of school, but it suddenly sank in that Columbia, Maryland, was not too far from the Pentagon, where many of their parents worked.

After presenting the idea for the book to my editors, I began thinking about the best people to contribute to it. Individual chapters are drawn from the vast experiences of these contributors, who were carefully selected based on their backgrounds. They have written diverse chapters based on their knowledge and insight. I began with the usual suspects; that is, librarians I have worked with on committees and on writing projects in the past. Kristine Mahood, booktalker extraordinaire, came to my mind first. Kristine and I met in 1995, when we were both young adult librarians in North Carolina—she in Salisbury, and myself halfway across the state, in Fayetteville. As members of the Young

Adult Committee of the Public Library Section of the North Carolina Library Association, we had quickly bonded. For a few years, we slaved away together while co-chairing the committee and producing a newsletter titled *Grassroots: For High Risqué Librarians*. I will never forget the day when Kristine called and told me that she had just accepted a position in the state of Washington. I did not realize it at the time, but one of the best mentors of my career was leaving. Since those faraway days, Kristine and I have pondered life, an anthropological study of librarians, and libraries on a regular basis. Kristine is currently a young adult librarian in Washington state, where she performs booktalks for teens in five counties, and is the author of *A Passion for Print: Promoting Reading and Books to Teens* (Libraries Unlimited, 2006). In *Serving Young Teens and 'Tweens*, she contributed a chapter about booktalking.

I met my second usual suspect, Robyn Lupa, when we were both members of the Young Adult Library Services Association (YALSA)'s Selected Films and Videos Committee in 1997. We became fast friends, mainly because we were the two youngest committee members. We spent many hours together, viewing and discussing videos during the American Library Association (ALA) midwinter meetings. Of course, we also took advantage of our free time in wonderful cities, managing to create our own parties in New Orleans, San Antonio, and Philadelphia. Since those committee days gone by, Robyn and I have relied on each other for humor, support, and encouragement. Robyn is the head of a children's services department in Colorado, previously served as a young adult librarian in New York, and has served on committees for both YALSA and the Association for Library Services to Children (ALSC). She contributed a chapter in this book on library programming.

Brenda Hager, a YALSA Serving the Underserved (SUS) trainer, has worked as a youth services librarian, serving both children and teens, in a public library in Maryland. She is currently an elementary school librarian, having direct contact with 'tweens on a daily basis. Brenda and I met at the 2001 YALSA SUS training in Washington, D.C., where we spent a few intense days learning about training adults to work with teens. As trainers, Brenda and I have presented in tandem to crowds of librarians in Maryland and Delaware, focusing on the developmental needs of youth. Brenda contributed a chapter on nonfiction resources.

Deborah Taylor, also a YALSA SUS trainer and a YALSA past president, is extremely knowledgeable about fiction for youth due to her involvement with the American Library Association. She has served on several book committees for both children and teens. Deborah and I have also conducted YALSA SUS training together, in both Delaware and Maryland. I have had the pleasure of seeing Deborah in action at a "Books for the Beast" conference in Baltimore, and I have sent young adult library staff to these excellent conferences as well. Deborah's chapter is on fiction for 'tweens and young teens.

Finally, there is James Rosinia. I first met James, formerly an employee at the Center for Early Adolescence in Chapel Hill, at a library conference in

North Carolina. At the time, I was inspired by his speech, and asked his permission to use the phrase "I stink and my feet are too big" for the title of an article I was writing for a library journal and for a staff training event at the Cumberland County Public Library & Information Center in Fayetteville, North Carolina. At the library conference where I met James, he had told a story about a teenager who described himself as smelling and having feet that were too big. James gladly agreed to write the foreword to this book, drawing upon his past experiences and his current position as the youth services consultant for the State Library of North Carolina.

When I interviewed for the position of library director at the Dover Public Library in Delaware, one of the interview questions was to describe any additional training that I have had besides my library education. One of my responses was that I had lived in various parts of the country, and although this was not actually "training," per se, it has taught me a lot about learning to work with various types of people from different geographical locations and backgrounds. Hence, this book is a compilation of some of those experiences. In my library career, I have had the opportunity to connect with people all over the United States. The book is enriched with information from authors who have lived and worked in various parts of the country, in libraries of different sizes, serving a variety of 'tweens and young teens.

Acknowledgments

I would like to thank all librarians who have provided sufficient materials for 'tweens and young teens. I am especially grateful to the staff at the West Deptford Public Library, New Jersey, and at the David A. Howe Public Library in Wellsville, New York, for making sure that 'tweens and young teens were a priority when I was growing up. I became a librarian because, as a young teen, I had access to books by Judy Blume, Ellen Conford, Robert Cormier, Chris Crutcher, Paula Danziger, M. E. Kerr, Norma Klein, Robert Lipsyte, Harry and Norma Fox Mazer, Richard Peck, and Paul Zindel.

Introduction

I hated being thirteen. I felt like an adult, but on the few occasions when someone was prepared to treat me like one, I screwed it up somehow!—(Cabot, Meg. "Kate the Great." In *13: Thirteen Stories That Capture the Agony and Ectasy of Being Thirteen*, edited by James Howe, 46. New York: Atheneum, 2003.)

'Tweens and young teens are a unique group of people who need individualized attention in a library setting. They do not always quite fit in when visiting the children's section at a public library, and they may not feel comfortable in an area for teens, either. Much like a high school senior, who might be suffering from senioritis, ready to move on to college, 'tweens and young teens may be eager to move into their teen years. Society has not always made this transition an easy one. Educators know this, and that is why junior high schools were changed into middle schools about twenty years ago. Parents tend to be more comfortable if their sons and daughters, who are still children in their eyes, are not yet exposed to high school life. Public libraries typically do not make this distinction once a child becomes a teen. To this day, there are few programs in libraries that are exclusively geared to young teens, and young people in this age group are often grouped together with teens who are older.

WHO ARE 'TWEENS AND YOUNG TEENS?

It is difficult to directly pinpoint the age range for 'tweens and young teens. Some consider 'tweens to be those between the ages of eight and twelve, whereas others consider young teens to be between ages thirteen and fourteen. Advertisers typically define the 'tween market in a particular way in order to sell products. In public schools, children and teens are usually segregated based on age into elementary school, junior high or middle school, and high school. Middle schools include students in fifth through eighth grade, or somewhere within the range of 'tweens and young teens. Homeschooled children and teens generally have another system for determining ages and grades, although many parents homeschooling their children and teens will rely on the same ages and stages as public schools in determining grade levels.

Physicians and other health care workers classify 'tweens and young teens based on physical development. This practice will differ throughout the world, for young people mature at variable rates due to differences in nutrition and genetics. Some young girls begin menstruating as early as nine, while some boys barely shave until age fifteen.

Public libraries also vary in how they define age categories, and typically they do not wish to be *in loco parentis*, relying on parents to determine what is appropriate for their son or daughter. However, young adult sections in public libraries do make distinctions in many cases. It is typical for a children's services department in a library to serve people ages twelve and under, but some libraries also include materials for middle school students in the children's area. Some libraries are so small that the separation between materials for different ages may only be distinguished by a shelf or two of various materials.

For the purposes of this book, the term "young teens and 'tweens" includes young people ages ten through fourteen. This range was chosen because youth this age vary greatly. While some girls in the early part of the range may already be menstruating, others may not have this experience until age thirteen or fourteen. Boys have growth spurts at different ages. Think about a typical sixth grade class, filled with a mix of people who look very young as well as people the same age who could pass for being much older. Both children and teens progress at different rates. There is diversity in development. In order to empathize with this age group, remain aware of the fact that all people need to be treated as individuals. Even when 'tweens and young teens visit the library in groups, remember that each person differs. Although you may witness a "mature" thirteen-year-old girl flaunting her developing body, keep in mind that the "immature" eleven-year-old boy, who may look as though he cannot be a day over seven, may be more mature on a mental level. In this scenario, someone unfamiliar with the stage of early adolescence may assume that the boy is immature and the girl is mature; it may be quite the opposite—looks are not everything.

WHY SERVE 'TWEENS AND YOUNG TEENS?

Public libraries in the United States typically base their services on a variety of specific criteria, including age groups. Children's librarians offer special services for toddlers, preschool-age children, and school-age children, tailoring collections and programs based on developmental needs. Adults, as well, are offered different services based on ages. Libraries have outreach programs for senior citizens who cannot physically visit the library. Other adults are offered unique services. For example, there might be an informational program held for newlyweds who are about to buy a house, or for adults who are reaching retirement and need to know more about financial matters.

The situation is usually different for young adult library services. Many librarians serving teens are forced to include all teenagers into one large age group, typically ages twelve or thirteen through eighteen, due to staff demands, space issues, and collection management. *Serving Young Teens and 'Tweens* gives practical suggestions for intentionally singling out a younger age group to meet their unique needs and demands as they grow through their teen years toward adulthood.

Librarians should be aware that 'tweens and young teens are at a stage in their lives when they may become less interested in the library. When people go through change of any sort (such as marriage, divorce, menopause, or retirement, for instance), they need information. 'Tweens on the verge of becoming teenagers are in a similar situation; they need to stay informed as they make choices about their lives. Just as 'tweens might decide that the library is not a cool place, they still need the services provided by the library. At this stage, librarians can intervene and help 'tweens to realize that the library is a worthwhile place to be. Librarians can support the independent learning skills that are beginning to develop in 'tweens. Many of these potential library users are likely to seek information, probably on the Internet. They realize that information is important, but without a positive adult influence promoting the library as a resource, these 'tweens and young teens might turn away from the library. Losing their patronage at this early stage can mean losing them for life.

AUDIENCE AND PURPOSE

The intention of this book is to help you, as a librarian, learn about what makes people in this age group unique from children, older teens, and adults; and to plan programs and services based on those needs. Whereas children's librarians are already accustomed to serving their clientele differently based on age, adult librarians have traditionally viewed young adults as one group. Just as a children's librarian understands that a toddler may need a board book about potty training, a young adult librarian needs to understand that 'tweens may need books about becoming a teenager.

Serving Young Teens and 'Tweens has been created for young adult librarians, children's librarians, and youth service workers who may be working with 'tweens and young teens in some capacity. This book can be used as a starting guide for serving this age group, or as a resource for improving existing services. When beginning any new project, it is important to know your audience. If you are trying to reach 'tweens and young teens, start first by understanding what makes them who they are. The developmental stages of adolescence are not complicated, but they are important, and everyone goes through them once in a lifetime. Once you know more about your audience, think about the collection that you currently have for this group in the library. Whether you are building a collection of fiction and nonfiction from scratch, or want to beef up your current collection of materials, there are many suggestions available in Chapters 2 and 3. Librarians unfamiliar with booktalking, and even those who are more seasoned, may be inspired by the booktalking suggestions given in Chapter 5. Offering 'tweens and young teens programs is a good way to keep them in the library, and to promote the library in a positive way. Youth familiar with children's programs will already be familiar with what the library can do for them, but try to reach out to those 'tweens and young teens who may be new to using the library as a form of recreation.

ABOUT THIS BOOK

In Chapter 1, "Childhood Left Behind: 'Tweens, Young Teens, and the Library," you will learn about the stages of adolescent development and how 'tweens and young teens are affected by hormones and their changing bodies. As 'tweens move from childhood to early adolescence, they are faced with cognitive and physical changes. Also in this chapter, you will find demographic statistics about 'tweens and young teens and their social world. When working with this age group, you may face special circumstances related to reference interviews, censorship, space concerns, and redirecting negative behavior. This chapter gives suggestions for handling these situations.

In Chapter 2, "And Knowing Is Half the Battle, When Entering the Zone: Nonfiction Resources for 'Tweens and Young Teens," Brenda Hager discusses the information needs of 'tweens and young teens, along with a thorough, annotated list of worthwhile nonfiction resources and library materials. She explains why it is necessary for 'tweens and young teens to seek information in the first place. Hager has carefully chosen topics meaningful to this age group, including friendship, religion, money, volunteering, hobbies, and physical fitness. She also explores nonfiction electronic materials, including online reference, software, chat rooms, electronic lists, and databases. Her chapter includes a thorough list of Web sites that will appeal to 'tweens and young teens. It also addresses writing, hobbies, health, and more. And, finally, Hager discusses possible collaborative efforts between school library media specialists and public librarians in providing the information needs of 'tweens and young teens.

Deborah Taylor, in Chapter 3, "Fiction for 'Tweens and Young Teens," explores the recreational reading needs of 'tweens and young teens, along with suggestions for fiction books, including many award winners, for this age group. She discusses youth development and how it relates to reading as well as social development, decision making, and problem solving. You will even find coverage of fictional books for 'tweens and young teens that are presented in unique formats, such as graphic novels and screenplays.

In Chapter 4, "Programming for 'Tweens and Young Teens," Robyn Lupa explains the importance of providing age-specific programs for 'tweens and young teens and suggests different types of activities that are appropriate for this group. Some of the topics for programs include books, education, games, celebrations, movies, and anime. Lupa explains the nuts and bolts of programming, including how to plan and promote programs, as well as reaching out to the community. There is information on how librarians serving teens can use the children's department as a resource.

Kristine Mahood gives practical advice for promoting books to 'tweens and young teens as well as sample booktalks in Chapter 5, " 'I Want to Read That Book!' Booktalking to 'Tweens and Young Teens." Her lists of carefully selected books that appeal to 'tweens and younger teens provide ready-made samples for use during school visits. Mahood also offers guidelines for booktalk visits, such as preparing mentally and physically for a booktalk performance, the importance of introducing oneself to the audience, promoting the library and library cards, and how to make the experience a memorable one for the audience.

CONCLUSION

In April 2006, Disney introduced a new product—cellular telephones specifically designed for young teens and 'tweens. The company decided to target parents who wanted to let their sons and daughters have cell phones but still have the power to control use and costs. The new phones are Disney-themed, and young teens and 'tweens can download Disney-related photographs and music. Parents can keep track of minutes and text messages. Like other industries and companies, Disney has identified the 'tween and young teen market as a sustainable economic force. Librarians can learn from Disney that this age group has sustainability in libraries as well, provided that they are given the services they need to make the library an attractive place.

1

Childhood Left Behind: 'Tweens, Young Teens, and the Library

Sheila B. Anderson

At the beginning of the twenty-first century, much popular culture is aimed not only at the whole 'tween and teen population, but at the whole range of adults, from young to old, as well.—(Graham, Philip, *The End of Adolescence*, p. 243.)

Kids these days are growing up faster. When I was young, I did not have to worry about the things that today's kids have to deal with. We did not have computers, electronic games, and ipods that exposed us to pornographic material, misinformation, and dangerous adults. The world was a safer place. Children played outside and walked to school. Toys that did not have to be plugged in were popular, and we typically played Kick the Can, touch football, and other games that required physical activity rather than sitting in front of a machine. We listened to regular radio and did not find it necessary to subscribe to satellite radio. In some towns, kids could come home for lunch in the middle of the day because one parent would be home. We knew our neighbors in days gone by, and we all looked out for each other.

How many times have you heard adults proclaim these remarks? Did you agree? Perhaps you have also heard adults say the opposite. They might claim that kids these days are better connected with society due to the availability of information. Maybe some adults even believe that the world is a safer place today compared to the past, due to technology such as cellular phone use, advances in medicine, such as DNA research, and the ability to keep track of people through web cams and other technology, such as micro-chips. Perhaps the neighbor who you may have relied on in the past to look out for your child is a registered sex offender, listed on a Web site that you have access to in your home or your library. Maybe you have heard adults defend toys that need to be plugged in, explaining the educational benefits of video games and various computer programs. Many children and young teens improve their eye-hand co-ordination by using computers and playing video games. I can name a few six-year-olds who would be great volunteers at the library, assisting senior citizens with using a computer mouse and other basic computer functions. Some youth have lost weight by playing video games that require them to move and dance, proving useful for those in need of physical activity. Whatever your beliefs, one can easily argue that times have changed, although we may disagree on whether it is for better or worse.

DEFINING 'TWEEN AND YOUNGER TEEN

A Tween is a combination of the words teen and in between. Your Tween is in between childhood and the teenage years—a time of exploration, growth, change, and turbu-lence. Any time one is in between, he or she is squeezed in the middle, and no one likes being in this uncomfortable position. (Corwin 1999, p. 1)

Since 'tweens and young teens reach different cognitive, physical, emotional, and social milestones at various times, it is difficult to pinpoint a specific range for this age group. There are cognitive, emotional, and social differences among youth of different ages, and during the preteen and teen years, these changes occur at different times. Whereas one eleven-year-old girl may begin menstruating and develop breasts, another may not reach this physical state until age thirteen. To cite another example, a thirteen-year-old boy may have reached his first nocturnal ejaculation, while an older youth of fourteen may not need to shave until he is well out of early adolescence. So it is difficult for librarians to pinpoint an exact time in a person's life when he or she can be called a 'tween or a young teen.

The diversity of these developmental phases and indeterminateness in re-gard to specific ages is reflected in the structure of library organizations that serve youth. For instance, the Young Adult Library Services Association (YALSA) of the American Library Association (ALA) defines its service population as those between the ages of twelve and eighteen. Those aged twelve are not necessarily teenagers, but an eleven-year-old girl may have already begun menstruating and is in the early stages of becoming a teenager. Through committee work, YALSA members create various booklists of materials appropriate for teens. The Asso-ciation for Library Services to Children (ALSC) of ALA defines their service area as those ages fourteen and under, and includes a reading list called "Great Middle Schools Reads" on their Web site. The Children's Book Council (CBC) Joint Committee, an ALA committee associated with ALSC, is another group that is concerned with both children and teens. The CBC produces lists of suggested books as gifts for youth in three categories, including young teens.

This overlap between library associations has resulted in some confusion and controversy. One such controversy has surrounded the age range for the Newbery Medal, which is awarded to books for young people ages fourteen and under, and the Michael L. Printz Award, which applies to books that span the ages of twelve through eighteen. Many years, the Newbery Medal is awarded to a book that is considered to be appropriate for teenagers, or both children and teenagers. Sometimes there is an overlap in the winners. For example, *Lizzie Bright and the Buckminster Boy* by Gary D. Schmidt was named a Printz Honor book in 2005. It was also named a Newbery Honor book that same year. The main character in this book, Turner Buckminster, is age thirteen. As another example, the book *Criss Cross* by Lynne Rae Perkins won the 2006 Newbery Award and was also named a YALSA Best Book for Young Adults that same year. *Criss Cross* describes the lives of four fourteen-year-olds in a small town as they discover the meaning of life.

When Mary K. Chelton was asked if she saw this overlap in book awards as a problem, she responded, "No. For better or worse, the children's and YA librarians both own that age group and they should talk to each other about it if the same book turns up on both lists. Young adolescents are all over the ballpark" (Firestone 2005, p. 105). Chelton further explained that young adolescents vary in their cognitive, physical, and social development, and that both children's librarians and young adult librarians should not fight over who owns the seventh grade, because they both do.

Likewise, within libraries, there is sometimes controversy as to which department should be serving which age groups. While managing the Young Adults' Services Department at the Allen County Public Library in Fort Wayne, Indiana, the Children's Services Department manager and I had a friendly agreement and we would let each other know about groups that may be more appropriate for our sections of the library. Her staff would provide storytelling to teens who were mentally disabled, and therefore cognitively at a younger level, while the Young Adults' Services Department gladly helped 'tweens who needed its services, such as those who were pregnant.

In *Hanging' Out at Rocky Creek: A Melodrama in Basic Young Adult Services in Public Libraries* (Scarecrow Press 1994), author Evie Wilson-Lingbloom focuses on young teens and services, stating that

> *Certainly, if a ten-year-old wants to check out a book from the YA Collection, she should be allowed to do so without judgment from the librarian...Many librarians consider the 9–11 age group to be an early adolescent group.*

> *Librarians who visit fourth grade classes to promote Summer Reading Clubs are likely to see a number of rolling eyeballs if their promotional materials are childlike! (pp. 3–4)*

In *Managing Young Adult Services: A Self-Help Manual* (Neal-Schuman 2002), author Renee Vaillancourt McGrath also explores the issues of services for teens of various ages:

> *Although there are benefits to grouping junior high or middle school students with high school students (particularly in the public library, where staff to serve each individual group are usually nonexistent), there may also be times when it is more appropriate to host programs that target a particular subset of "young adult" only. (p. 28)*

DEVELOPMENTAL STAGES OF EARLY ADOLESCENCE

> *It was on my chin. A little bit right of center. It's funny how I knew it was a pimple the instant I saw it. I mean, why didn't it occur to me it could be a measle? Or cancer? Anything else. But no, I just knew it. Without even thinking. Teenage instinct, I guess. (Spinelli 1982, p. 86)*

In this excerpt from *Space Station Seventh Grade*, Jason describes what it was like to find a pimple on his face and how he copes throughout the school day. This scene is familiar to many 'tweens and young teens. Like many other authors, Spinelli is a master at explaining what seventh grade is like, and vividly describes how bodies can change during puberty. In the early stages of adolescence, 'tweens and young teens experience physical, cognitive, and social changes.

Physical Changes

> *Everything I knew about sex then—which was a lot—came from books from a local suburban library. I started reading about sex when I was 9 (fourth grade). I took children's and adolescents' books about sex out of the library on my mom's card. (Friday 1991, p. 484)*

It may be astonishing to some adults, including librarians, that a child as young as nine is curious about sexuality and has taken the initiative to use the public library to find information about it. Some librarians may feel pleasantly surprised to know that youth are using library resources to find such important information. Other librarians may become a bit alarmed, wondering where the parental responsibility lies in the entire process of youth and access to information through library materials. Yet others, who have remained in tune with the times, may not be so surprised. Perhaps they have read the results of the National Campaign to Prevent Teen Pregnancy's report surveying twelve-, thirteen-, and fourteen-year-olds. The 2003 data states that one in five teens has had intercourse before age fifteen, and that contraceptive use among young adolescents is low (Lally 2003).

During the course of a natural progression toward adulthood, childhood will be left behind. Thus, it is imperative that you, as a librarian, are prepared to serve youth who are in a difficult stage of life, leaving childhood and entering their 'tween and teen years. By remaining open minded about providing necessary services to this population, and by becoming familiar with their developmental needs, you can help youth make a smoother transition out of childhood.

Being able to hide physical changes during the 'tween and young teen years is not an easy task. Many young teen boys are embarrassed about the occurrence of erections at inopportune moments, and girls are often ashamed to have breasts or menstrual periods, especially if some of their classmates still do not. Also, many 'tweens and young teen girls wonder when their periods will finally begin. Girls mature before boys, typically beginning around ages ten and eleven, when they experience a growth spurt. Their breasts begin to develop and pubic hair begins to grow. Underarm sweat begins to develop around age twelve or thirteen, and most girls begin menstruating between ages eleven through fourteen. Some girls, however, begin menstruating earlier or later—even as late as sixteen. Girls need to be prepared for these physical changes, and parents are not always involved in the process. In some cases, parents willingly assist girls with learning about the basics of growing up—such as how to use tampons, how to sit properly while wearing a skirt, or how to choose a bra. Other children who are about to become teenagers do not learn what they need to know at home and may need more support. This is why access to information, either in print or electronic media, is so vital for youth at this age.

Boys experience a growth spurt at ages twelve or thirteen. Testes enlarge at this time, and boys experience ejaculation at age thirteen or fourteen. Pubic hair begins to grow at age eleven or twelve while facial hair typically does not appear until a boy is between ages thirteen and fifteen. Voices begin to deepen at about age fourteen or fifteen. Boys also need access to information that is accurate, up-to-date, and unbiased. Although youth will typically learn about growing up from their peers and, sometimes, older siblings, the information is not always correct and the public library needs to be a place youth can rely on for unanswered questions.

There has been a lot of research on the disadvantages of early development. Some girls who develop early are faced with situations that are difficult to handle, such as being approached by older boys, or even men who assume that they are older based on their physical development. It is not unusual to see girls who develop at an early age keeping their arms crossed in front of their chests when they are in public. Girls who develop later may also feel self-conscious because they have not kept pace with their peers. This is a time when changing in the locker room for gym may be extremely difficult. Boys who develop at an early age are typically larger than their peers. Although this can be seen as a benefit for male athletes, it may also mean being shunned or criticized by adults who do not understand why they are acting so "immature"—despite the fact that they may only be age twelve or thirteen. Because their cognitive abilities have not caught up with their bodies, they still may act immature. Male 'tweens and young teens who develop later may be prone to teasing due to their smaller size and lack of a need to shave. This can also be painful for the boys, as it may also cause problems in locker rooms and other locations where they cannot hide the fact that they have not yet matured into a teenager.

Cognitive Changes

> The brain of a young person is a work-in-progress—
> tremendous progress. The period between ages nine and ten
> and early adolescence is marked by dramatic neurological
> growth and change. The only other time in life when the
> human brain achieves such strides is the period soon after
> infancy. (Ginsburg and Jablow 2002, p. 32)

'Tweens and young teens begin to think in more advanced ways as they grow into adulthood. According to Piaget's Theory of Cognitive Development, young people ages eleven and older are in a stage of "formal operations," meaning that they are able to develop abstract and hypothetical reasoning. Unlike children, who are typically limited to thinking about what is real, 'tweens and young teens are able to begin thinking about what is possible. They can consider hypothetical situations. They can think about abstract things, and they are getting better at arguing. This is a time when they are likely to criticize library policies and procedures. It is important for library administrators to create extremely clear policies for this reason. Young teens are also likely to think about the process of thinking. They are better able to reason; and this typically causes conflicts with adults and other authority figures. At this stage, 'tweens and young teens are very egocentric, thinking that the world evolves around them. Young adolescents are also better able to process information compared to their childhood years. They are better able to pay attention. As they age, their memory improves, assisting with their ability to solve problems.

Social Changes

> "High expectations" has become a cliché today, but their
> importance for young adolescents cannot be overempha-
> sized. Why? Because by fifth or sixth grade, kids are more

sensitive to what others think of them—and more likely to believe those assessments—than they will ever be again. (Stepp 2000, p. 168)

'Tweens and early teens are expanding their circle of acquaintances, not relying on parents and siblings as much for social interaction. During this time, they perceive their parents to be aliens and are typically embarrassed by them. This is evident at the library when a 'tween or young teen will make faces or hide when visiting with a parent who has done something that is not appropriate, in their eyes, such as saying the wrong words or, heaven forbid, touching them on the shoulder or patting them on the top of their head, for instance. Friends become important to 'tweens and teens because it is the beginning of their social world. They quickly form cliques in schools in junior high and middle school, which generally creates even more tension in an atmosphere that is already stressful.

During these years, friendships may form that last a lifetime. Consider the musicians Paul Simon and Art Garfunkel:

Paul becomes friends with fellow sixth-grader Art Garfunkel during rehearsals for a class production of Alice in Wonderland; they bond over a mutual interest in music and discover they can harmonize. By the mid-'50s, the inseparable duo performs at high-school dances and parties, their vocals accompanied by the acoustic guitar Paul got on his 14th birthday. (Martindale 2003, 24)

Milestones of Early Adolescence (Adapted from Fenwick and Smith 1996)

1. Worries about appearance of developing body, resulting in self-consciousness

2. Hormonal changes, resulting in moodiness

3. Asserts independence, resulting in an attempt to find a separate identity

4. Rebellious and defiant behavior, resulting in demands for more freedom and rudeness

5. Friends become more important, resulting in the need to identify with friends

6. Needs to belong to a peer group and feel a sense of belonging, resulting in friends becoming supreme

7. Sees issues from his or her own view, but has a strong sense of justice, resulting in intolerance and difficulty in compromising

Other friendships may only last a short time and may change on a daily or hourly basis. This is typical during the 'tween and young teen years when interests and hobbies are bound to change rapidly.

Today, many 'tweens and young teens rely on technology for socializing. It is not unusual for this age group to have cellular telephones, PDAs, ipods, and computers. In public libraries, many enjoy instant messaging each other, even if the person they are sending a message to is sitting right beside them. With the availability of text messaging via cellular phones, as well as the ability to send photographs and videos, 'tweens and young teens are better able to keep in touch with their friends. While 'tweens and young teens of days gone by would compare the colors of their sneakers or friendship bracelets, the newer generation compares ring tones and screen savers that they have downloaded.

DEMOGRAPHICS OF 'TWEENS AND YOUNG TEENS

Consider national statistics relating to young teens as a broad base for learning about this segment of the population. Remember, however, that each community is different, and it is worthwhile to become more familiar within your library service area. Also, be aware that researchers are not likely to define "young teens" as they are being described in this book; most likely, practitioners will break down statistics about young teens based on whether they are in middle or high school, and if they are under or above age twelve. Therefore, it is sometimes difficult to find statistical figures that directly relate to 'tweens and young teens.

Births to Young Teens at Lowest Levels in Almost 60 Years

- Birth to young adolescents aged 10 to 14 has fallen to the lowest level since 1946.

- The number declined from a peak of 12,901 in 1994 to the current low of 7,315.

- In 2000, two-fifths of pregnancies among 10- to 14-year-olds ended in a live birth, two-fifths ended in induced abortion, and one in five ended in a fetal loss.

- Non-Hispanic black (1.9 per 1,000) and Hispanic adolescents (1.4 per 1,000) had the highest rates of pregnancy in 2002.

- The U.S. birth rates among young teens ranged from a low of .2 per 1,000 in Maine to a high of 2.0 in Mississippi and the District of Columbia.

Births to 10- to 14-Year-Old Mothers, 1990–2002: Trends and Health Outcomes at www.cdc.gov/nchs.

Normal Adolescent Development

Early Adolescence (12–14 Years)

Movement toward Independence

Struggles with sense of identity

Moodiness

Improved abilities to use speech and express oneself

More likely to express feelings by actions than by words

Close friendship gain importance

Less attention shown to parents, with occasional rudeness

Realization that parents are not perfect; identification of their faults

Search for new people to love in addition to parents

Tendency to return to childhish behavior, fought off by excessive activity

Peer group influences interests and clothing styles

Career Interests

Mostly interested in present and near future

Greater ability to work

Sexuality

Girls ahead of boys

Same-sex friends and group activities

Shyness, blushing, and modesty

Show-off qualities

Greater interest in privacy

Experimentation with body (masturbation)

Worries about being normal

Ethics and Self-Direction

Rule and limit testing

Occasional experimentation with cigarettes, marijuana, and alcohol

Capacity for abstract thought

Reproduced from the Center for Adolescent Studies, Indiana University (http://education .indiana .edu/cas/adol/development).

Total Population Projections by Sex and Age

	2005	2010
Males 10–14 years	10,670,000	10,109,000
Females 10–14 years	10,167,000	9,658,000

Source: Statistical Abstract of the United States: National Data Book, 2004–2005 (Washington, DC: GPO), p. 13.

Resident Population by Race, Hispanic Origin, and Age: 2003
Age 10–14

White	16,192,000
Black or African American	3,145,000
American Indian, Alaska native	270,000
Asian	769,000
Native Hawaiian and other Pacific Islander	45,000
Two or more races	503,000
Hispanic or Latino origin	3,661,000
Non-Hispanic White	12,857,000

Source: Statistical Abstract of the United States: National Data Book, 2004–2005 (Washington, DC: GPO), p. 16.

Resident Population by Race, Hispanic Origin, and Age
Age 10–14

	2005 Projections	2010 Projections
White	15,881,000	15,049,000
Black	3,332,000	2,976,000
Asian	787,000	834,000
Other races	838,000	909,000
Hispanic origin	3,853,000	4,057,000
Non-Hispanic White	12,370,000	11,361,000

Source: Statistical Abstract of the United States: National Data Book, 2004–2005 (Washington, DC: GPO), p. 18.

Computer and Internet Use by Children and Adolescents: 2001

	Age 8–10	Age 11–14
Total children	12,455,000	16,493,000
Use computers at school	83.1%	85.2%
Use computers at home	62.7%	68.6%
Use word processing at home	23.8%	42.1%
Connect to the Internet at home	39.5%	54.1%
Use e-mail at home	23.9%	43.3%
Complete school assignments at home	37.7%	56.6%
Play games at home	54.0%	62.9%

Source: Statistical Abstract of the United States: National Data Book, 2004–2005 (Washington, DC: GPO), p. 160.

Profile of Consumer Expenditures for Sound Recordings—Percent Distribution: 1990–2003

Age 10–14	
1990	7.6%
1995	8.0%
1998	9.1%
1999	8.5%
2000	8.9%
2001	8.5%
2002	8.9%
2003	8.6%

Source: Statistical Abstract of the United States: National Data Book, 2004–2005 (Washington, DC: GPO), p. 724.

LEARNING ABOUT 'TWEENS AND YOUNG TEENS

During the preadolescent years, girls are typically happy, interested in sports or other activities, and they talk freely with their parents. As adolescence progresses and as peer pressure mounts for experimentation with drugs, alcohol, and sex, many girls draw away from their parents, are tempted into destructive behavior, and in the process lose their sense of self. (Carbone 2006, p. 469)

In her book *Last Dance on Holloday Street*, Elisa Carbone describes what life was like for girls in a brothel during the nineteenth century in the American West. Today, girls as young as nine are being lured into prostitution. This phenomenon has occurred with middle-class youth in places like Minnesota in the Mall of America, where young girls are lured by pimps, according to Suzanne Smalley, author of "This Could Be Your Kid," published in the August 18, 2003, issue of *Newsweek*.

Surprised? The best way to learn about 'tweens and young teens is to begin by looking at the past and then concentrate on the future. You might not need to go all the way back to the nineteenth century, though. Simply think about your own life when you were between eleven and fourteen. What made it difficult? What did you dread the most? Enjoy the most? I dreaded lunch in the fifth grade when everyone was segregated at tables based on cliques. I typically worried about getting lost or forgetting my locker combination, and to this day, I still have nightmares that I am trapped in the halls of my middle school, trying to find my classroom. Regarding good memories, mostly as a young teen, I enjoyed writing, reading, and swimming. So start by thinking back to your own teen years. As a YALSA Serving the Underserved (SUS) trainer, I have learned that empathy is important in helping adults remember their own teen years, and to sympathize with teens in the library.

Movies and television shows have featured 'tweens and young teens, but the portrayal is not always accurate, so do not make general assumptions based on what is shown on the big screen. Think about *Malcolm in the Middle*. Does he seem realistic to you? The movie *Mean Girls* is based on the book *Queen Bees and Wannabees*, and is supposedly authentic regarding how girls treat each other during the early teen years.

When the movie *Thirteen* was released, there was a lot of controversy regarding the content. The screenplay was written by older teens who were reflecting back on their early teen years. Some viewers did not believe that the destructive behavior of the characters—using drugs, being sexually active, stealing, and engaging in mutilation—was realistic. According to Evan Rachel Wood, the movie focused on "really screwed-up teenagers" (Puig 2003).

Another way to learn about 'tweens and young teens is to read about them. Start with your local newspaper to find out what is happening in your own community. Next, branch out to state and national sources, such as using online databases to find out trends within this age group. This method will allow you to have tons of information about them, including facts about physical, social, emotional, and cognitive issues. For instance, you may be surprised to learn that advertisers are paying young teens and 'tweens to try out and promote their products. 'Tweens and young teens, believe it or not, are sometimes big spenders. You may learn that young teens are drinking large amounts of caffeine, which may not always be good for them.

In your research you may discover that 'tweens and young teens are even more in tune with technology than most people realize. The popular Web site Myspace.com has caused controversy, with adults fearful that predators are targeting 'tweens and young teens via the Web site. In fact, Nick Lachey, formerly the husband of Jessica Simpson, launched Yfly.com, a Web site similar to Myspace.com, for young teens. "Lachey says he got behind Yfly after

A Chronology of Landmark Books about 'Tweens and Young Teens

1970 *Bless the Beasts and Children* (Glendon Swathout)

1973 *A Hero Ain't Nothing' but a Sandwich* (Alice Childress)

1975 *Dragonwings* (Laurence Yep)

1979 *Words by Heart* (Ouida Sebestyen)

1983 *A Solitary Blue* (Cynthia Voigt)

1984 *The Moves Make the Man* (Bruce Brooks)

1987 *Hatchet* (Gary Paulsen)

1989 *Shabanu: Daughter of the Wind* (Suzanne Fisher Staples)

1993 *Shadow Boxer* (Chris Lynch)

1995 *The Eagle Kite* (Paula Fox)

1997 *The Facts Speak for Themselves* (Brock Cole)

1999 *When Zachary Beaver Came to Town* (Kimberly Willis Holt)

2000 *Holes* (Louis Sachar)

2001 *The Rag and Bone Shop* (Robert Cormier)

2002 *My Heartbeat* (Garret Freymann-Weyr)

2003 *13: Thirteen Stories That Capture the Agony and the Ecstasy of Being Thirteen* (edited by James Howe)

2004 *Al Capone Does My Shirts* (Gennifer Chaldenko)

2004 *Contents Under Pressure* (Lara Zeises)

2005 *Click Here (To Find Out How I Survived Seventh Grade)* (Denise Vega)

2006 *Here Lies the Librarian* (Richard Peck)

learning that his identity is one of those most frequently used by predators to lure teens. A December poll of 1,468 teens by the Polly Klaas Foundation found half have exchanged messages with someone they don't know" (Hempel 2006).

Another way to learn about 'tweens and young teens is to immerse yourself in literature that has been written for them. Well-written realistic fiction for teens typically focuses on the characters, portraying their lives accurately. The publishing industry for young teens and 'tweens is in full throttle; just ask

Travy van Straaten, director of publicity for Simon & Schuster Children's Publishing. Van Straaten organized a "tween tour," featuring authors D. Anne Love, Rachel Cohn, and Frances O'Roark Dowell, who all write for this age group (Lodge 2003). The authors, from three different states, visited bookstores and schools, read from their novels, answered questions, and signed books.

SPECIAL CONSIDERATIONS IN SERVING 'TWEENS AND YOUNG TEENS

Collection Development and Censorship Issues

> Dr. Wick seemed utterly innocent about American culture, which made her an odd choice to head an adolescent girls' ward. And she was easily shocked about sexual matters. The word fuck made her pale horse face flush; it flushed a lot when she was around us. (Kaysen 1993, pp. 84–85)

A concerned parent brought to my attention that the book *Girl Interrupted* by Susanna Kaysen, featuring an eighteen-year-old protagonist, was in the young adult section. This parent felt that the book was too mature for her thirteen-year-old daughter due to its sexual themes. I explained that the young adult section included materials for a large age range and that it was the responsibility of the parent to decide what the daughter should read. I also supplied reviews of the book and pointed out that the book was nonfiction and was actually an autobiography. After supplying the reviews, I did not hear from the parent again. The book, which was made into a movie with actresses Angelina Jolie and Winona Ryder, is the true story of the author's time in a mental institution after she graduated from high school in the late 1960s. Throughout the book and the movie, the main character refers back to difficult events that occurred during her high school days—and some of the reasons why she ended up in the mental institution in the first place.

For some thirteen-year-olds the book may not be appropriate; but it is the role of the parent, not the public librarian, to make that determination. The article "What They're Reading on College Campuses" in the June 2, 2000, issue of *The Chronicle of Higher Education* lists *Girl Interrupted* as the second most popular book read on campus, after *The Hours* by Michael Cunningham and before *Beowulf*, translated by Seamus Heaney. The other books on the list include *The Cider House Rules* by John Irving, *Woman: An Intimate Geography* by Natalie Angier, *The Testament* by John Grisham, *American Psycho* by Bret Easton Ellis, *Harry Potter and the Sorcerer's Stone* by J. K, Rowling, *Tuesdays with Morrie* by Mitch Albom, and *The Poisonwood Bible* by Barbara Kingslover. The list was derived from information given by stores serving college and university campuses throughout the United

States. Many of the popular titles may have been popular with older teens in the year 2000, and some are assigned reading in high school. Most public libraries keep all young adult materials for people of various teen ages together, and sometimes the classics are also kept in the young adult section. It is not unheard of, therefore, for materials read on the college level to be appealing to younger people. Some books, such as those by J. K. Rowling, are typically kept in all sections of the library—adult, teen, and juvenile—since they have crossed generational boundaries and have become highly popular with various age groups.

Much of fiction that is produced for young adults concerns issues related to social problems. Realistic fiction, earlier known as the "problem novel," addresses topics that are not always easy to swallow, such as death, homelessness, sexuality, suicide, and violence. In the summer of 2000 and in fall 2005 I taught a graduate course in young adult literature. I was not surprised, in both 2000 and five years later, that my students found young adult literature to be too bleak. Many commented that the literature seemed depressing and that teens probably needed an outlet that was cheerful, especially with so much chaos being portrayed in the news media. In order to assist my students with taking a closer look at realistic fiction, I assigned them to read the article "Raining on the 'Rainbow Party'" by Joy Bean, published in the April 25, 2005, issue of *Publisher's Weekly*. The article criticizes the book *Rainbow Party* by Paul Ruditis and raises concerns that the book features young teens who are involved in parties where oral sex is the main focus. The book has caused some commotion throughout the library world, with many librarians thinking more deeply about collection development issues and youth, especially young teens.

Since parents are more likely to bring censorship challenges to librarians when their children are in either kindergarten or middle school, it is apparent why some books alarm many concerned parents. With a thorough collection development policy, though, and a staff that is familiar with the library collection, these issues may not be as difficult. The staff should be well trained to respond to censorship issues. Some library directors want to handle any concerns about censorship, while others rely on their frontline staff to respond to problems as they occur. One option is to begin by thanking the parent for being concerned enough about the welfare of their child to bring the issue to the attention of the staff. Of course, you need to smile sweetly while doing this, and that is a task that sometimes cannot be learned. Next, explain that the public library services the needs of the entire community and that other people might want to read that particular book. It is sometimes helpful to remind the parent that, unlike a school situation, public librarians are not responsible for creating collections that reflect curricular needs.

Most of all, make sure that you are familiar with the collection, procedures for collection development, and any policies that may be in place. Be prepared to answer questions from the public (as well as officials, and perhaps the media) regarding how materials are selected for the library. Make it clear that staff members are very careful when selecting materials and that they use reviews from library journals as a tool for selection. If the library staff uses other means for selection, such as popularity according to Web sites like amazon.com, this should be mentioned to anyone unhappy with library materials.

One of the basics of librarianship is having a clear, well-written collection development policy that has been approved by whoever funds, or is responsible for, the institution. For example, in Dover, Delaware, the library is a city department, and the Dover City Council approves the library's collection development policy. In other public libraries where the library board of trustees has more power, they may be the people responsible for approving the policy. In a school library, a board of education may approve collection development policies. The policy should describe the collection; explain how decisions are made regarding purchases; detail guidelines for gifts, donations, and weeding; and include a reconsideration of materials form. Most libraries have opted to adopt the ALA's Library Bill of Rights as part of the collection development policy. This can be used to support a library's claim to intellectual freedom should unreasonable complaints arise.

Despite having a clear collection development policy and being an advocate for intellectual freedom, the headaches associated with censorship challenges might not go away. The Office for Intellectual Freedom of the ALA gives excellent advice and provides plenty of resources, but it still cannot completely solve issues within local jurisdictions. In preparation for possible censorship issues, make sure that you are familiar with the collection and that you can justify its existence. This is true not only for the teen collection but also for the entire collection. Does your library own *How to Make Love Like a Porn Star: A Cautionary Tale* by Jenna Jameson? If not, why? It was on the *New York Times* best seller list for a significant amount of time. The book is Jameson's autobiography, starting with her porn star career beginning at age sixteen. She went from being a high school cheerleader to a stripper and a nude model, and, finally, to a porn actress while becoming addicted to crack cocaine. The book may not be appropriate for all communities, some librarians may argue, while others may strongly believe that any book that is included on such a prestigious best seller list should be available in all public libraries. The point is that librarians need to become familiar with what they are purchasing for their collection.

It is important that your library include a large selection of materials for 'tweens and young teens, as well as for older teens. The reading levels of people this age will vary greatly; whereas some 'tweens and young teens may still be reading books by the children's author Beverly Cleary, others may have already progressed to hard-core science fiction by adult authors. Publishers typically determine the age range for certain materials, and this information can be found by using reviews in library journals. Remember that most teens, especially 'tweens and younger teens, who want to read about older people, love reading magazines. Keeping a stocked shelf of typical teen magazines, as well as some magazines that are intended for adults, will result in a lot of library traffic.

Please refer to subsequent chapters in this book in order to find more specific information on building fiction and nonfiction collections for this age group.

Space Issues

The first stop is Tech Central, an installation of 40 computers for tweens. Staffed by a five-member technology education team, Tech Central provides software for learning and recreation, as well as Internet access for those with parental permission. (Kenney 2005)

ImaginOn is a joint venture with the Public Library of Charlotte & Mecklenburg County and the Children's Theatre of Charlotte. It is a mix between a museum, a library, and a theatre. There is a separate children's room, a "Story Lab," a "Teen Loft," and "Tech Central" specifically for 'tweens to learn about library research, database searching, PowerPoint, Dreamweaver, and more. This nontraditional library reaches youth of all ages. The Teen Loft has books, magazines, and graphic novels. The Tech Central is unique in that it is a technology center specifically geared toward 'tweens and young teens. Books and other materials appropriate for youth are located in the same building, so 'tweens and young teens have choices of many different materials that are age-appropriate.

The physical location of various materials for 'tweens and young teens within a library is a concern among library staff and parents. Most public libraries do not have a section of materials for this age group. Some libraries keep materials for middle school students in a separate section, or include it in the children's department but in a different area within the department. This is the case in the Bel Air Branch of the Harford County Public Library in Maryland and the Carmel Clay Public Library in Indiana. Some libraries are so small, or cramped for space, that the only materials that are teen-specific are housed on a shelf or two, usually nestled in an adult area or a children's area.

Reference Interviews

Think about the last time that you were in an important meeting at work, or were involved in a memorable family gathering and felt as though you were being scrutinized for one reason or another. All eyes were on you, your mouth became dry, and you felt as though you were on fire while you experienced a slight ringing in your ears. Your face was perhaps either beet red or white as a ghost, depending on the circumstances. Whatever the case, you were extremely uncomfortable at that particular moment.

'Tweens and young teens often feel like they are under scrutiny from everyone, including any authority figure as well as the general public. Since they are naturally self-centered at this age, they falsely believe that everyone is paying attention to them. They are extremely self-conscious, and it is often difficult for them to approach the reference desk in a public library to ask questions. They may feel heat rise into their heads while walking into a library, anticipating a stressful situation. Many times, they will unsuccessfully attempt to find information themselves and will never approach a staff member for help. They may feel stupid when asking questions, and they typically believe the notion that librarians know everything.

As a librarian, there are steps that you can take to make reference transactions less painful for yourself and the 'tween or younger teen. Remember that body language is important, so start by smiling. Do not hide behind your desk. Pointing is a problem for most patrons, and for 'tweens and younger teens, it is even more so. They may be too scared to ask for help again if they did not understand where you have directed them to go. Also avoid giving too much information during reference transactions. Many times, 'tweens and young teens may be in a rush and only need specific information rather than a plethora of resources. Since 'tweens and young teens vary in size and physical maturity, try not to judge based on appearance. As an eager young adult librarian, I remember suggesting that a library patron join our summer reading program. The parent stepped in, explaining that her daughter was only nine, but an early bloomer. This was, of course, embarrassing for both the parent and the child, and an eye-opening experience for me as a new librarian. Speaking of parents, many times it is difficult for librarians to talk directly to a 'tween or a young teen due to aggressive and overbearing parents. If you are trying to determine homework assignments, or to dig deeper regarding a reference question, sometimes it is not easy to get the parent to back off.

As a YALSA SUS trainer, I also caution librarians about asking the teens if a reference question is a homework assignment, adding that "The twelve-year-old who is asking about abortion might actually need one." Of course it is useful for reference librarians to know about upcoming homework assignments, but staff should not make assumptions about questions that are asked at the reference desk, particularly when it concerns a sensitive topic. Librarians should respect all questions, from patrons of any age, but especially 'tweens and young teens who probably had difficulty approaching a public service desk in a library. Remember that maintaining confidentiality is a standard ethical issue in librarianship, and minors also have a right to privacy when using the library.

Wandering around the library stacks is a good way to approach patrons who may be reluctant to ask a question at a public service desk. Due to security reasons, librarians should identify themselves as a staff member first. It is important to maintain a casual tone, but not too casual—remember that even 'tweens and young teens will see right through an adult who is not acting in an age-appropriate manner or is trying to act too "cool" during reference transactions. 'Tweens and young teens might be more likely to ask for assistance in the stacks, where they do not feel they are on display in an open public setting. This may allow for better service in the long run.

Redirecting Negative Behavior

Scenario: You are sauntering through the YA area of the library, and something strange and drastic has just occurred. You stand there wondering what has overcome your body in such a debilitating way. Ah, you finally realize the problem: your senses have become temporarily disabled. The smell of bubble gum, strawberry lip gloss, and the combination of smelly sneakers and body odor could nauseate the strongest of librarians. A thirteen-year-old girl is flaunting shorts that you *know* she was not wearing when she left her house. A twelve-year-old boy is strutting around in a T-shirt that says, "I'm Wearing This to Annoy You." Many four-letter words are being whispered, there is gossip of who's dating who, and page 115 of Judy Blume's book *Forever* is being recited by memory. You have just entered the puberty zone, otherwise known as "hormone hell." (Rapp 1998, p. 2)

In libraries, it is not at all unusual to see 'tweens and young teens hanging out. At this age, they need positive interaction with adults who understand their developmental needs, especially related to social growth. When training librarians to work with teenagers, I have often used the passage above to illustrate what it is like to encounter 'tweens and young teens in public libraries. Most young adult librarians realize that it is natural behavior for people this age to travel in packs, to huddle together, and to ignore the rest of society. This may result in a lot of loud noise and commotion. When approaching a group of rowdy 'tweens and young teens, keep in mind that since they are egocentric, they probably do not even realize that they are being loud. Try to redirect negative behavior by making sure that the library offers productive activities, such as programs and volunteer opportunities.

It is necessary to be consistent with rules. If you have rules in the library about certain behaviors, and you only enforce them on occasion, teens will respond in a negative manner. Keep in mind that libraries are not necessarily quiet environments, as they were in the past, and that some noise may need to be tolerated. If your library director does not spend any time on the front lines, make sure that your managers relay information to the library director and other administrators about problems that arise. It may be possible to change rules that are not necessary in order to improve customer service. Of course, this will depend on the culture of your individual institution, as well as the attitudes of the decision-makers.

Sometimes it is more productive to address rowdy groups as a whole, and other times, depending on the circumstances, you may want to pull the leader of the group aside and explain the problem. Often, a more responsible teen who is with a group of disruptive teens will leave the group before the trouble boils over. When approaching disruptive 'tweens and young teens, do not make threats; state the consequences in a clear manner. For example, if teenagers are throwing paper on the floor, you may want to offer choices, saying, "You have two choices. You can either clean up the mess that you made, stop throwing paper, and stay in the library. Your other choice—if you continue to throw paper—is to leave the library right now, and you cannot return until tomorrow." Also, carry out what you say you are going to do; for instance, if the consequence of the action is that you will ask the teens to leave if they are not quieter, and they continue to be noisy but you do not ask them to leave, you have lost your credibility.

Keep in mind that when 'tweens and young teens visit the library after school, they are usually bursting with energy. Typically, they have been sitting in school all day, and in the public library they are expected to continue sitting in a chair—not running up and down the steps, playing on the elevator, crawling on the floor, making out in the corner, or doing cartwheels in the aisles. When I was a young adult librarian in North Carolina, my coworkers and I would suggest to rambunctious young men that they consider running around the block a few times before entering the building again in order to burn off some steam.

PROFESSIONAL RESOURCES

> *Until very recently, we made little distinction between the early elementary years and the later elementary years, from about age eight to twelve. The new awareness of the special needs of this group is best shown in the emergence of the term tweenagers, signifying that these children are not kids in the sense that they were a few years ago, nor are they ready to be treated as teenagers. (Sullivan 2005, p. 24)*

Within professional literature, some librarians have segregated information about serving children and teens based on ages. *Fundamentals of Children's Services* by Michael Sullivan includes information about serving tweenagers, including detailed information on administering book discussion groups for this age group.

In *Young Adults and Public Libraries: A Handbook of Materials and Services* (Greenwood Publishing Group 1998), edited by Mary Ann Nichols and C. Allen Nichols, the chapter "Adolescent Development: An Emotional Roller Coaster" by Melanie Rapp addresses the developmental differences of adolescents. *Center Stage: Library Programs That Inspire Middle School Patrons* by Patricia Potter Wilson and Roger Leslie (Libraries Unlimited 2002), although focusing on school media centers, provides a plethora of ideas for programming with middle school students that are both educational and recreational. Some of the suggestions include storytelling, health, art, games, puzzles, holidays, and poetry. In *Bare Bones Young Adult Services: Tips for Public Library Generalists* (American Library Association 2000), the author focuses on the stages of adolescent development and notes that young teens are especially clumsy and self-conscious.

Lucille W. Van Vliet's *Media Skills for Middle Schools: Strategies for Library Media Specialists and Teachers* (Libraries Unlimited 1999) gives advice for orienting middle school students, provides suggestions for programs, and describes characteristics of middle school students. In *Do It Right! Best Practices for Serving Young Adults in School and Public Libraries*, the authors focus on social myths, stating,

> *Early adolescence is a period of development second only to early childhood in velocity. Many different changes occur simultaneously within the individual, but at different rates of growth—physical, social, emotional, psychological, cognitive, etc. In practical terms, this means that adult service providers, who frequently judge solely—and incorrectly—by appearance, cannot use this yardstick with this age group."*
> *(Jones and Shoemaker 2001, p. 3)*

Some library resources focus directly on developing collections for 'tweens, young teens, and middle school students. As an example, *Best Books for Middle School and Junior High Readers: Grades 6—9* by John T. Gillespie and Catherine Barr (Libraries Unlimited 2004) includes a thorough list of materials appropriate for this age group. Library journals that offer reviews of materials often suggest an age group. These typically include middle school, junior high, high school, or adult books that will appeal to teenagers. *Voice of Youth Advocates*, for example, defines middle school as grades sixth through eighth, junior high as grades seventh through ninth, senior high as grades tenth through twelfth, and adult-marketed books recommended for YAs. Each review includes a code that determines the audience for the material.

Voice of Youth Advocates also has a booklist in each February issue, titled "Top Shelf Fiction for Middle School Readers," featuring material that is appropriate for people ages eleven through thirteen or in grades sixth through eighth. Since 2000, librarians and educators have served on a committee to create the booklist. Graphic novels, popular with all ages, are also making their way into the hands of 'tweens and young teens. "Graphic Novels: for Tween Girls," published in the February 2006 issue of *Teacher Librarian*, gives suggestions of graphic novels for young girls.

Sandra Hughes-Hassell, associate professor at the College of Information Science and Technology at Drexel University, and Christina Lutz, a Drexel University graduate student, conducted research on the leisure reading habits of urban middle school students, which was featured in the Winter 2006 issue of *Young Adult Library Services.* The study tracked why middle school students like to read, or why they do not read; and what they like to read about, including celebrities, animals, musicians, and more. The researchers found that most middle school students like to read for fun, and when they do not read, it is because they would rather watch television or spend time with their friends (Hughes-Hassell and Lutz 2006).

Many books are available to assist adults with understanding young adolescents. The books listed below are not exclusively meant for librarians, but can be generally useful in learning more about teens. Some of these books have been specifically created for 'tweens and young teens, but parents, educators, librarians, and other adults might profit from them by becoming more empathetic toward this age group and by learning what life is like for 'tweens and teens.

Campbell, Ross. **How to Really Parent Your Teenager: Raising Balanced Teens in an Unbalanced World.** New York: W Publishing Group, 2006.

Provides advice on keeping communication open between teens and parents, dealing with depression and rebellion, and discussing sexuality.

Canfield, Jack. **Chicken Soup for the Preteen Soul: 101 Stories of Changes, Choices, and Growing Up for Kids Ages 9–13.** Deerfield Beech, CA: Health Communications, 2000.

Includes stories about growing up, in order to help tweens and young teens transform into their teen years.

Clifford-Poston, Andrea. **Tweens: What to Expect from—and How to Survive—Your Child's Pre-Teen Years.** Oxford: Oneworld Publications, 2005.

Packed with case studies about young teens, who are growing up more rapidly, both physically and mentally.

Corwin, Donna G. **The Tween Years: A Parent's Guide for Surviving Those Terrific, Turbulent, and Trying Times between Childhood and Adolescence.** Lincolnwood, IL: Contemporary Books, 1999.

Includes information about physical milestones, emotions, school, anger, discipline, problem solving, sex, substance abuse, depression, and eating disorders.

Dellasega, Cheryl, and Charisse Nixon. **Girl Wars.** New York: Fireside, 2003.

Shows how to stop adolescent girls from hurting each other with cruel words and insensitive actions.

Ezzo, Gary. **Preteen Wise: Parenting Your Child from Eight to Twelve Years**. New York: Henry Holt, 1999.

Provides advice to parents on preparing for the teen years. The book is chock full of quizzes for parents and questions at the end of each chapter. A section called "The Sex Talk" gives advice to mothers and fathers on talking to their preteens about sex.

Giannetti, Charlene C., and Michael J. Killins. **What Are You Doing in There? Balancing Your Need to Know with Your Child's Need to Grow.** New York: Broadway, 2003.

Tackling the frustrations and fears of parenting in a world where cyber predators make headlines and "normal" adolescents act out in ways that beg the question, "Where are the parents?" Presents a new way of approaching a child's private life.

Ginsburg, Kenneth R., and Martha M. Jablow. **"But I'm Almost 13!" An Action Plan for Raising a Responsible Adolescent.** New York: Contemporary Books, 2002.

Helps parents help their young teens deal with stress, peer pressure, and more.

Hartley-Brewer, Elizabeth. **Talking to Tweens: Getting It Right before It Gets Rocky with Your 8 to 12 Year Old.** Cambridge, MA: Basic Books, 2005.

Provides advice to parents on understanding 'tweens, discipline, morals, friendship, health, sex, puberty, family problems, drugs, drinking, and education. There are lists of useful tips throughout the book, including tips on the effective use of punishment, responding to shoplifting, tidy bedrooms, quality time, manners, homework, exams, and talking about sex.

Jackson, Anthony W. **Making the Most of Middle School: A Field Guide for Parents and Others.** New York: Teachers College Press, 2004.

Describes developmental stage of early adolescence, explains middle schools, how teachers can make a difference, explores safe schools, how parents can be involved in the education of their middle schoolers, and gives resources for parents.

Kaplowitz, Paul. **Early Puberty in Girls.** New York: Ballantine, 2004.

What it is, how it happens, when to be concerned, and how it should be treated. Written by a leading pediatric endocrinologist.

Mosatche, Harriet S., and Karen Unger. **Too Old for This, Too Young for That: Your Survival Guide for the Middle-School Years.** Minneapolis, MN: Free Spirit, 2000.

Explores health, privacy, families, dating, time management, and peer pressure with examples of problems and how to solve them. The book is interspersed with hot lines, Web sites, booklists, cartoons, and questionnaires.

Panzarine, Susan. **A Parent's Guide to the Teen Years: Raising Your 11 to 14 Year Old in the Age of Chat Rooms and Navel Rings.** New York: Checkmark Books, 2000.

   Explores the physical, emotional, and cognitive changes faced by those in the stage of early adolescence. Gives suggestions for handling problems that are typical for this age group.

Perlstein, Linda. **Not Much Just Chillin; the Hidden Lives of Middle Schoolers.** New York: Ballantine, 2004.

   The author spent nine months immersed in the lives of five suburban MD middle school students and writes about her experience.

Rainey, Barbara, and Dennis Rainey. **So You Want to Be a Teenager? What Every Preteen Must Know about Friends, Love, Sex, Dating, & Other Life Issues.** Nashville, TN: Thomas Nelson, 2002.

   From a fundamentalist Christian point of view, gives advice about life, love, and sex.

Rosenberg, Ellen. **Get a Clue! A Parents' Guide to Understanding and Communicating with Your Preteen.** New York: Owl Books, 1999.

   Provides practical advice to parents about raising preteens, covering topics such as puberty, sex, and social issues.

Shure, Myrna B., and Roberta Isrealoff. **Raising a Thinking Preteen: The "I Can Problem Solve" Program for 8 to 12-Year-Olds.** New York: Henry Holt, 2000.

   Assists parents with helping preteens learn to solve problems and conquer issues such as conflicts with family and friends.

Sonna, Linda. **The Everything Tween Book: A Parent's Guide to Surviving the Turbulent Preteen Years.** Avon, MA: Adams Media Corporation, 2003.

   This thorough book helps parents understand the developmental stage of early adolescence and gives advice on solving issues with growing up.

Stepp, Laura Sessions. **Our Last Best Shot: Guiding Our Children through Early Adolescence.** New York: Riverhead Books, 2000.

   Explores the results of in-depth interviews that the author conducted with young teens for two years.

Wiseman, Rosalind. **Queen Bees and Wannabees: Helping Your Daughter Survive Cliques, Gossip, Boyfriends, and Other Realities of Adolescence.** New York: Three Rivers Press, 2003.

   Provides parents with advice on how to help their daughters cope with adolescence. The movie *Mean Girls* is based on this book.

Zodkevitch, Ron. **The Toughlove Prescription: How to Create and Enforce Boundaries for Your Teen.** New York: McGraw-Hill, 2006.

This guidebook helps parents enforce rules related to common behavior problems.

CONCLUSION

'Tweens and young teens are at an age when they are beginning to break free from their parents and other adults who have had an influence on their lives. They are beginning to rely more on information from their friends and others who are not part of their immediate circle of family and acquaintances. This can be a painful time for parents as they realize that their babies are growing up, and it can also be difficult for adults, such as teachers and librarians, who may be struggling to understand why 'tweens and young teens sometimes have bursts of energy and are interested in the world, and, at other times, are sullen and need to be left alone. The more you learn about this group, the better you will be prepared to serve them.

WORKS CITED

Bean, Joy. "Raining on the 'Rainbow Party.' " *Publishers Weekly* 252, no. 7 (April 25, 2005): 28.

Carbone, Elisa. "From Dance Halls to Malls: Saving Girls' Sense of Self." *Voice of Youth Advocates* 28, no. 6 (February 2006): 468–469.

Corwin, Donna G. *The Tween Years: A Parent's Guide for Surviving Those Terrific, Turbulent, and Trying Times between Childhood and Adolescence.* Chicago: Contemporary Books, 1999.

Fenwick, Elizabeth, and Tony Smith. *Adolescence: The Survival Guide for Parents and Teenagers.* New York: DK, 1996.

Firestone, Tracey. "Inside the Librarian's Studio with Mary K. Chelton." *Voice of Youth Advocates* 28, no. 2 (June 2005): 105.

Friday, Nancy. *Women on Top.* New York: Simon & Schuster, 1991.

Ginsburg, Kenneth R., and Martha M. Jablow. *"But I'm Almost 13!" An Action Plan for Raising a Responsible Adolescent.* Chicago: Contemporary Books, 2002.

Gorman, Michele. "Graphic Novels: For Tween Girls." *Teacher Librarian* 33, no. 3 (February 2006): 22.

Graham, Philip. *The End of Adolescence.* Oxford: Oxford University Press, 2004.

Hempel, Jessi. "A Cool but Safe Hangout?" *Business Week,* no. 3967 (January 16, 2006): 11.

Hughes-Hassell, Sandra, and Christina Lutz. "What Do You Want to Tell Us about Reading? A Survey of the Habits and Attitudes of Urban Middle School Students toward Leisure Reading." *Young Adult Library Services* 4, no. 2 (Winter 2006): 39–45.

Jameson, Jenna. *How to Make Love Like a Porn Star: A Cautionary Tale.* New York: Regan Books, 2004.

Jones, Patrick, and Joel Shoemaker. *Do It Right! Best Practices for Serving Young Adults in School and Public Libraries.* Teens @ the Library Series. New York: Neal-Schuman, 2001.

Kaysen, Susanna. *Girl, Interrupted.* New York: Vintage, 1993.

Kenney, Brian. "Imagine This: Charlotte's ImaginOn Takes a Radical Leap into the Unknown." *School Library Journal* 51, no. 12 (December 2005): 53–55.

Lally, Kathy. "Sexual Experience before 15." *Baltimore Sun*, May 21, 2003, 2A.

Lodge, Sally. "Tales from the Tween Tour." *Publisher's Weekly* 250, no. 19 (May 2003): 27–28.

Martindale, David. "Biography: Paul Simon." *Biography* 7, no. 12 (December 2003): 24.

Perkins, Lynne Rae. *Criss Cross.* New York: Greenwillow Books, 2005.

Puig, Claudia. "Thirteen Is Teen Extreme." *USA Today*, September 17, 2003.

Rapp, Melanie. "Adolescent Development: An Emotional Roller Coaster." In *Young Adults and Public Libraries: A Handbook of Materials and Services*, edited by Mary Ann Nichols and C. Allen Nichols. Westport, CT: Greenwood Press, 1998.

Smalley, Suzanne, Joseph Contreras, and Sarah Childress. "This Could Be Your Kid." *Newsweek* 142, no. 7 (August 18, 2003): 44–47.

Spinelli, Jerry. *Space Station Seventh Grade.* New York: Little, Brown, 1982.

Stepp, Laura Sessions. *Our Last Best Shot: Guiding Our Children through Early Adolescence.* New York: Riverhead Books, 2000.

Sullivan, Michael. *Fundamentals of Children's Services.* Chicago: American Library Association, 2005.

Vaillancourt, Renee J. *Bare Bones Young Adult Services: Tips for Public Library Generalists.* Chicago: American Library Association, 2000.

"What They're Reading on College Campuses." *Chronicle of Higher Education* 46, no. 39 (June 2, 2000): A14.

FOR FURTHER READING

Albert, Bill, ed. "14 and Younger: The Sexual Behavior of Young Adolescents." *The National Campaign to Prevent Teen Pregnancy.* Washington, DC, May 2003.

Aldercise, Kit. "Chick Lit for Teens and Tweens." *Publishers Weekly* 251, no. 46 (November 15, 2004): 24–26.

Aurther, Kate. "The Awesome Tales of the Tweens." *New York Times Magazine* 154, no. 53299 (August 7, 2005): 26, special section.

Baker, Sharon L., and Karen L. Wallace. *The Responsive Public Library: How to Develop and Market a Winning Collection.* Westport, CT: Libraries Unlimited, 2002.

Barson, Michael, and Steven Heller. *Teenage Confidential: An Illustrated History of the American Teen.* San Francisco: Chronicle Books, 1997.

Brown, Robert, and Ruth Washton. *The U.S. Market for Tweens and Young Teens: Attitudes, Aspirations, and Consumer Behavior of 8 to 14 Year Olds,* 3rd ed. New York: Market Research, 2005.

Burr, Ty. "Teenage Wasteland: Do You Know What Your Kids Are Up To? 'Thirteen' Paints a Not-So-Pretty Picture." *Boston Globe* (Boston, MA), August 29, 2003, C1.

Campbell, Patty. "Middle Muddle." *Horn Book Magazine* 76, no. 4 (July/August 2000): 483.

Cohen, Jonathan. "Friends Again." *Billboard* 115, no. 38 (September 20, 2003): 6.

Collins, Clayton. "Marketers Tap Chatty Young Teens, Hit a Hot Button." *Christian Science Monitor* 97, no. 87 (March 30, 2005): 11.

Cox, Ruth. "Preteen and Young Teen Protagonists." *Teacher Librarian* 31, no. 2 (December 2003): 16.

Donelson, Kenneth L., and Alleen Pace Nilsen. *Literature for Today's Young Adults,* 7th ed. New York: Longman, 2005.

Ebert, Patrice. "Young Adolescents and Libraries: Summary of Program Presented at 1985 NCLA Conference." *North Carolina Libraries* 43 (Winter 1985): 217–218.

Edmunds, Gail A. "Sensitivity: A Double-Edged Sword for the Pre-Adolescent and Adolescent Gifted Child." *Roeper Review* 27, no. 2 (Winter 2005): 69.

Engberg, Gillian. "On the Verge: Puberty in Fiction about Girls." *Booklist,* June 1, 2005, 1790.

Farmer, Lesley. "Collection Development in Partnership with Youth: Uncovering Best Practices." *Collection Management* 26, no. 2 (2001): 67–78.

Gardner, Marilyn. "Do Adults Understand Young Teenagers' Needs?" *Christian Science Monitor* 92, no. 152 (June 28, 2000): 19.

Glasser, William. *For Parents and Teenagers: Dissolving the Barrier between You and Your Teen.* New York: Quill, 2002.

Havris, Kathryn L. "Relieving the Junior High Jitters: Public Library Program for Future Junior High Students and Their Parents." *Voice of Youth Advocates* 15 (April 1992): 15–16.

Hegna, Kristinn. "Older Adolescents' Positive Attitudes toward Younger Adolescents as Sexual Partners." *Adolescence* 39, no. 156 (Winter 2004): 627.

Heppermann, Christine M. "Laughing in the Face of Puberty: Books about Sex." *The Horn Book* 76, no. 2 (2000): 162–168.

Holt, Glen. "Library Branding for Young Adolescents: Learning from Barbie and Mickey." *The Bottom Line* 16, no. 2 (2003): 76–78.

Hughes-Hassel, Sandra, and Jacqueline C. Mancall. *Collection Management for Youth: Responding to the Needs of Learners.* Chicago: American Library Association, 2005.

Johnson, Peggy. *Fundamentals of Collection Development & Management.* Chicago: American Library Association, 2004.

Jones, Patrick. *New Directions for Library Service to Young Adults.* Chicago: Young Adult Library Services Association, 2002.

Jones, Patrick, Michele Gorman, and Tricia Suellentrop. *Connecting Young Adults and Libraries: A How-to-Do-It Manual*, 3rd ed. New York: Neal-Schuman, 2004.

Jones, Patrick, Patricia Taylor, and Kirsten Edwards. *A Core Collection for Young Adults.* New York: Neal-Schuman, 2003.

Kang, Stephanie. "Not a Kid, Not an Adult: What Kind of Consumer Electronics Do 'Tweens' Want? Toy Makers Are Determined to Find Out." *Wall Street Journal*, April 25, 2005, eastern edition, R4.

Kelly, Marguerite. "Helping a Child Enter the Teen Years." *The Washington Post*, June 20, 2001, C12.

Kennedy-Ross, Selicia. "Teen Novels Take Turn toward Risque." *The Sun* (San Bernardino, CA), September 22, 2005.

Kerr, Barbara A., and Sanford Cohn. *Smart Boys: Talent, Manhood, & the Search for Meaning*. Scottsdale, AZ: Great Potential Press, 2001.

Kleiner, Carolyn. "The Littlest Freshman of All." *U.S. News & World Report* 127, no. 11 (September 20, 1999): 54.

Knowles, Elizabeth, and Martha Smith. *Boys and Literacy: Practical Strategies for Librarians, Teachers, and Parents*. Westport, CT: Libraries Unlimited, 2005.

Lesesne, Teri. *Naked Reading: Uncovering What Tweens Need to Become Lifelong Readers*. Portland, ME: Stenhouse, 2006.

Lewin, Tamar. "1 in 5 Teenagers Has Sex before 15, Study Finds." *New York Times*, May 20, 2003, print media edition, late edition (East Coast), A18.

Lipper, Joanna. *Growing Up Fast*. New York: Picador, 2003.

Maggio, Mary. "Romancing the Young Teen." *Voice of Youth Advocates* 18, no. 6 (February 1996): 360–362, 367.

Manlove, Jennifer, Kristin Moore, and Janet Liechty. "Sex between Young Teens and Other Individuals: A Demographic Portrait." *Child Trends*. Child Trends, Inc., Washington, DC, November 2005.

Maughan, Shannon. "Betwixt and Be'tween." *Publishers Weekly* 249, no. 45 (November 11, 2002): 32.

Maxym, Carol, and Leslie B. York. *Teens in Turmoil: A Path to Change for Parents, Adolescents, and Their Families*. New York: Viking, 2000.

Meltz, Barbara F. "Middle School Cliques: A Common Challenge." *Boston Globe*, September 27, 2001, H8.

Moore, Nancy. "'We Were Reading Geography Books! I Thought We Were Just Reading for Fun': Parents and a Librarian Take on Seventh Grade Book Groups." *Voice of Youth Advocates* 22, no. 5 (December 1999): 310–312.

Myers, Arthur Solomon. "'Are You Afraid to Die?' 7th Graders Confront AIDS." *Voice of Youth Advocates* 19 (February 1997): 312–314.

Office for Intellectual Freedom. *Intellectual Freedom Manual*, 7th ed. Chicago: American Library Association, 2005.

Orr, Tamra. *Violence in Our Schools: Halls of Hope, Halls of Fear*. New York: Franklin Watts, 2003.

Paulu, Nancy. "Helping Your Child through Early Adolescence: For Parents of Children from 10 through 14." Washington DC:

Department of Education, Office of Intergovernmental and Interagency Affairs, August 2002.

Ponton, Lynn. *The Sex Lives of Teenagers: Revealing the Secret World of Adolescent Boys and Girls.* New York: Dutton, 2000.

Riera, Michael, and Joseph Di Prisco. *Field Guide to the American Teenager: A Parent's Companion.* Cambridge, MA: Perseus, 2000.

Sagarse, Margaret. "Letters; Meannness Has to Do with Age, not Sex." *Los Angeles Times*, May 15, 2002, E3.

Setoodeh, Ramin. "13 Going on 17." *Newsweek* 143, no. 21 (May 24, 2004): 12.

Shreve, Jenn. "The Hidden Lives of Middle Schoolers." *Instructor* 115, no. 1 (August 2005): 37–39.

Sim, Leslie, and Janice Zeman. "Emotion Regulation Factors as Mediators between Body Dissatisfaction and Bulimic Symptoms in Early Adolescent Girls." *Journal of Early Adolescence* 25, no. 4 (2005): 478–496.

Snyderman, Nancy L., and Peg Streep. *Girl in the Mirror: Mothers and Daughters in the Years of Adolescence.* New York: Hyperion, 2002.

Steinberg, Laurence. *Adolescence*, 7th ed. New York: McGraw Hill Higher Education, 2004.

Taffel, Ron. *Breaking through to Teens: A New Psychotherapy for the New Adolescence.* New York: Guilford Press, 2005.

Tauber, Michelle. "Young Teens & Sex." *People* 63, no. 4 (January 31, 2005): 86–93.

Trestrail, Joanne. "Science Explains Teenage Brain: A Run of Risky Behavior Can Drive Parents Mad." *Chicago Tribune*, September 16, 2001, 5.

Vaillancourt, Renee J. *Bare Bones Young Adult Services: Tips for Public Library Generalists.* Chicago: American Library Association, 2000.

Valenza, Joyce Kasman. "What about Reading?" *School Library Journal* 49, no. 9 (September 2003): S10.

White, Emily. *Fast Girls: Teenage Tribes and the Myth of the Slut.* New York: Scribner, 2002.

2

And Knowing Is Half the Battle, When Entering the Zone: Nonfiction Resources for 'Tweens and Young Teens

Brenda Hager

I was at that age when boys suddenly change from a boy to, well, not a man, but something in-between the two—a demented, terrifying creature known as an adolescent.—(Meyer, Stephanie H., and John Meyer, eds. *Teen Ink 2: More Voices, More Visions.* Deerfield Beach, FL: Health Communications, 2001, 278.)

INFORMATION NEEDS

Most of us have been there: a young man walks up to you and asks for some help, but he is at that age when you are just not sure—is he still a child or is he a teenager? One of the first things we do as children's librarians or young adult librarians is to assess his age and maturity level. Will you need to lean down to help this child and use terms that are simplistic and useful to his world? Or do you need to act a little more "cool" because he has just entered his senior year and has *clearly* learned everything there is to know about libraries, and the human race for that matter? But no, you think to yourself, this young man does not quite look tall enough or mature enough to be a teen yet—he might still be in middle or elementary school. Yes, he is in the *ZONE*, the "I'm not really a teenager yet, but I'm not a child anymore" zone. And you have the daunting task of helping him find what he needs! Do you use your very scripted reference interview that is *sooo* far from being teen friendly? Perhaps with the added difficulty of trying to gather information for a younger teen who is not even quite sure what being a teen is yet? Well, fortunately, it does not have to be this hard for public and school librarians. There really are a lot of great nonfiction resources out there for younger teens—you just have to step back into their world and think about what they need in their everyday lives.

So let us go back . . . I was already thirteen and taller than most of my girlfriends at my middle school in Colorado. I was sure there was something wrong with me. Why was it that all of my girlfriends had already gotten their first periods and mine was taking so long? It just did not make sense to me! Although my mother said that it would come when my body was ready, it had not! I would often think, like the main character of Judy Blume's (1970) famous teen story, "Are you there God? It's me, Brenda, and I'm having some issues down here you need to help me out with." I just knew people could tell, they were looking right at me and I could see it in their eyes, they must be thinking, "She is clearly the only one in the middle school who hasn't gotten her period!" I could see it in their faces and expressions, and clearly my only option at that point would be to lie about the situation and pretend I had already started my period if I planned to have any chance of maintaining respect in my school. This is certainly not the case for every teen, but, developmentally, younger teens do begin to think that everyone is looking at them, and they are convinced that if they are not totally in sync with what others are experiencing, there must be something wrong!

So what did I do? I read every book and magazine I could get my hands on that told me about what I would be going through. This was to help me mask the truth when others asked me about the situation. But guess what; I simply learned a lot about what would finally happen. That need for information was real and I breezed through the resources with ease. However, did I have the best resources available to me? I would often flip through youth and teen magazines to gain understanding. A recent study published in *Adolescence* found that younger teens read mass media women's magazines, gaining some unrealistic views of their bodies and feeling unhealthy dieting pressures (Thompson, Weber, and Brown 2002). Younger teens need to have a wide spectrum of information available to them and not simply rely on resources that can influence developing young minds with a particular commercial advertising slant. Feminists are concerned that teens do not get an accurate portrayal of their options and also miss necessary, more accurate, information about sex and sexual practices if they only read magazines such as *Seventeen* (Kaplan 2003). And surely this is not the only group concerned with this popular form of information access.

So Why Do Teens Read and Seek Information?

I just gave an example of an information need I had as a younger teen, but I probably did not recognize it as such. Reading usually begins as a way to experience a story, but from birth we are beginning to figure out our world. We take in information through various means. Play and interaction with others is how it all begins, but we then learn to read, which allows us one more channel through which information can arrive. Throughout the early years of school, we must learn to not only read the words but also to make sense of the language we are deciphering. "Reading to become informed" is how it is often stated in the world of education, but this is truly what we hope children will begin to learn early on and throughout the middle school years. As caring adults and professionals, we hope they experience this more enriched form of reading and gathering information. Catherine Snow states in her report, *Researchers Outline Elements Needed to Achieve Adolescent Literacy,* "Somewhat neglected in those various efforts [to improve early-reading achievement] was attention to the core of reading: comprehension, learning while reading, reading in the content areas, and reading in the service of secondary or higher education, of employability, of citizenship." Ms. Snow, in the foreword of the report, writes: "Educators must thus figure out how to ensure that every student gets beyond the basic literacy skills of the early-elementary grades, to the more challenging and more rewarding literacy of the middle and secondary school years" (Manzo 2004). We must then encourage every young teen to think critically and continually ask questions about their reading and knowledge, leading them to seek more understanding through better resources.

We are hopeful that younger teens are at this stage of being able to branch out from their younger reading to the more developmentally appropriate and challenging texts that will prepare them for the future, emotionally and cognitively. Scientists previously thought that brain mapping occurs mostly during the first years of life, but more recent brain research suggests that there is actually a second wave of gray matter expansion during teenage years. This may explain why teens often misinterpret emotional expressions of others and make poor decisions compared to older teens who are more able to predict (Spano, 2003). Reading literature that prepares them for potential choices and outcomes, rather than hearing advice from an adult, also grants them the independence to make their own well-informed and healthy choices. You may recall Brenda Dervin's "Sense Making Model" from library school. This access model of new information truly fits into a young teenager's situation. Their information gap or barrier (information need) is then bridged by the uses or helps (the information they receive, no matter what format). Ross J. Todd, director of the Research Center for International Scholarship in School Libraries, Rutgers University, suggests that this framework truly lends itself to helping information professionals assess the needs of younger teens (Todd 2003). Because of their inability to fully predict outcomes, younger teens can come to a hopeful solution or gain the knowledge needed for their tomorrows.

PONDERING TOMORROWS

To-morrow, and to-morrow, and to-morrow, Creeps in this petty pace from day to day, To the last syllable of recorded time; And all our yesterdays have lighted fools; The way to dusty death. Out, out, brief candle! (Shakespeare, Macbeth*)*

Unlike Macbeth stating that life is just a shadow across time, younger teens often cannot wait to experience tomorrow. They want to "get there," but may have a bit of anxiety about what is coming or just how they might get there. They want to learn about all aspects of what their tomorrows will entail. What will their bodies experience? What will school be like? How will they ever make friends in high school? How can they ensure that they will become popular, stay popular, avoid popularity? Possibly, they may want to erase themselves from the face of the earth so they will not have to go to high school.

Come on, think back. Remember when you walked into your high school for the first time and thought, "There is no way I am ever going to remember where my classes are?" It only takes a second to slip back into that world and begin to connect with what young teens are going through today. Make sure you are in this world when you are looking for resources for your teen areas. What do they want to know? If you cannot figure it out, ask them. Researchers and reading specialists identify a new trend they like to call "screenage" rather than teenage. This term describes teens' lives in a world of digital technology. Educators, librarians, and publishers need to recognize that the reading interests and behaviors of our adolescents have changed forever in this digital world. This is a key factor in trying to hook these reluctant readers.

So at this age, we have several factors coming together at once: natural curiosity about more abstract ideas, physical changes, cognitive growth in understanding and processing information, and a natural rebellion or breaking away from dependence on adult information. Young teens are ready to discover truths and process information on their own. So when you are faced with assisting that next young man who is in the ZONE with an information need, you will be able to assist and guide him in gathering and processing materials to answer his questions.

GROWTH IN NONFICTION AND TECHNOLOGY

As a society, we are more open than past generations to educating our young people about what is happening to them now and tomorrow. This is evidenced by the classes that younger teens are taking, the Web site information available, and certainly the growth in this area of publishing for younger teens.

Writersweekly.com currently offers a writing course for those interested in writing for new lucrative audience of teens and 'tweens ages 7–12. "Cash in on

Teens and Tweens in this six-week writing course," they state. And there is a lot out there to choose from when using this Web site.

So why such a big boom in publishing for these younger teens, or what we sometimes refer to now as " 'tweens?" Well, the truth is that in years past, the publishing industry paid more attention to stories for younger teens (Carter 2000). Companies then realized that there was an audience of older teens looking for something before reading adult books. Now teens have access to so much information in a variety of modes that it is important for us as information professionals to ensure that the information is age appropriate. Dr. James U. McNeal, president of McNeal & Kids, Youth Marketing Consultants, states that teens ages 8–12 are approximatley 20 million strong, and earn or are allowed about $22.68 a week, making up a $23 billion dollar market. He compares this number to $6 billion only a decade ago (McNeal 2001). Publishers and manufacturers respond to the needs and wants of this age group with plenty of books and products.

Information Access Tools of Tomorrow

Something to watch for in the future is the wave of personal devices that are evolving into the all-in-one entertainment, communication, and information access tools of tomorrow. Kids and teens were asked to name the things they would most like to have as back-to-school necessities. Based on some of their answers, the trends of the future include information that comes in forms integral to other types of resources, rather than separate input media forms. If you use technology, you know it is frustrating to have to carry and keep track of several different devices, such as a cell phone, a PDA, and an MP3 player. Teens want these devices to keep up with news, sports, music, games, and to stay in touch with family and friends. The trends of today and the near future, according to this poll, are up-and-coming devices that are evolving to meet this market.

As information professionals, are we keeping up with the electronic information needs of young people? Do you know what a thumb drive is? Have you set up your bluetoothing yet? What was your latest music or book download? Have you participated in any blogging or podcasting lately? A blog, short for Web log, is defined as an online diary or journal entries posted on the World Wide Web (World Book 2006). Podcasting involves using computers and computer technology tools to create and broadcast programs using the Internet rather than radio waves. Further descriptions and instructions on this are available at http://epnweb.org (Weinberger 2006).

These could both become very popular communication tools for young teens, but as librarians we should see a red flag here: it is important that young teens recognize the reliability concerns inherent in this mode of information exchange. You may have heard of the new Smart Watch that teens are all asking for? Some students in elementary school are now using PDAs or personal digital assistants. These may even be devices that are combined with their phones and MP3 players. Although teens are often not anxious to schedule their lives in ways that adults do, companies are creating software that can help them keep organized in school. The Smart Watch allows teens to download information like news bites, scores, weather information, and horoscopes. Some even offer instant messaging. USB memory devices, also known as thumb drives, are seen on many younger teens today. Some may not even recognize the older 3½ floppy disks that we were used to. Companies are very aware of the market for preteen electronic devices. Prior to the 2005 holiday season, Disney announced their production of an MP3 player made specifically for the preteen audiences. According to an article published by CNET News.com (Dawn 2005), companies like Hasbro and Disney are creating MP3 players to compete with the already existent ipod appeal to young teens.

Make sure the information they gather from your library's books or databases is storable on these devices (Chezzi 2004). What does your Web site look like on a pocket PC? Do you need to change your coding so that they can access the information you provide from their digital devices? It is important to keep up with these changing needs and plan for future technology changes with your budget. If students spend time in your library researching and creating a document or project on your computers, they would be very disappointed to learn that they cannot save it. Many also use free e-mail services, and they are not able to store or send much information or large documents via these free tools.

School Library Media Specialists and Public Librarians

If you are a school library media specialist you are not only encouraged to embrace new technology, but are also often required to do so. This is especially the case if your school district is purchasing the latest in information access and communication technology. You will be left behind if you do not educate yourself on these tools. However, you might be with a district that still uses only audio cassettes and VHS tapes to relay audio and visual information to your students, and may have no idea when you will be able to mix MP3 technology in with your students' information access. Regardless at what level you are able to serve, it is likely that the students are not waiting for you or the school to catch up with their information needs. Stay ahead of the game by connecting with what your public library offers, or get to know your local public librarians who serve the same population as you. This is not a one-way street; public librarians should also be reaching out to the media specialists who guide their customers during school hours. It can be as simple as an e-mail alert to the public librarians that your students might be coming with certain needs, or that you have reccomended they go to the public library for a particular assignment. The public librarian may have a swarm of young teens arriving with the same assignment in hand. If there are no open lines of communication, both the librarian and the students will certainly be frustrated when the students return with negative attitudes because they were overwhelmed or frustrated by the lack of resources, available technology, or professional assistance. So, before you become dissapointed each time they arrive with the same assignment or return on Monday with no resources, make the phone call, send the e-mail, or post the assignment. State the requirements of the assignment and the strategies you are reinforcing with information literacy so that the public library staff are aware. Public librarians, keep the phone numbers of the media specialists on your desk or create an address list with your e-mail program to keep the communication open in order to better serve this population, and be proactive when it comes to creating lifelong learners. Do not forget: we have very similar goals for our young developing users.

Forming Partnerships

As a school library media specialist and a former public youth services librarian, I put the public library phone number, Web address, and other contact information on our library media welcome brochure, which is distributed to students and staff. Additionally, when I collaborate with a teacher on a research project, I suggest the public libraries as a resource on their assignment handouts in order to ensure that they have every opportunity to stumble into their public library for additional rich resources and excellent professional assistance. Some programs across the county are much more involved and have formal partnerships between the public libraries and school libraries. School librarians already have the skills and knowledge to collaborate professionally, so why not also build these bridges with others in your field to support the need for information literate students? Create a formal partnership between the school district's school library media program and public library system. Have both parties agree to the partnership and make it something that is feasible for staff, finances, and time. You do not want to bite off more than you can chew, or your partnership will fail. Clarify whether you are simply going to notify each other of projects and happenings for younger teens, or if you are going to share services such as homework help programs, which can be extension services of programs and assignments from the school. Before the school doors shut for the summer months, ask yourself if you have worked with the local school or the local public librarians on compiling the summer reading lists and creating oportunities for young teens to foster their reading needs. Many times staff on both ends of the spectrum are "reinventing the wheel" and duplicating lists that could easily be combined to meet a common goal. For a list of great partnership ideas and partnership awards, log on to YALSA's Professional Devleopment Center at http://www.ala.org/ala/yalsa/profdev/schoolpublic.htm. or PLA's Web site http://www.ala.org/ala/pla/plaissues/earlylit/partnerships/garrison.ppt#1.

SUGGESTED RESOURCES

The following is an annotated list of selected resources that may be helpful in serving young adolescents. The books vary from the general to the more specific, depending on their individual subject area and are only a small sample of the variety of books related to these topics available to younger adolescents. Each book has an accompanying annotation following the bibliographic information, which will give you an idea of the overall scope of the book.

Growing Up Has Never Been Quite Like This

The following bibliography is a list of books that could fit the information needs of younger teens, as well as parents and professionals working with them. Most librarians are aware that there are differing opinions on how much a younger teen needs to know concerning sex, sexual practice, puberty, and dating. I have tried to include a range of resources that can satisfy a variety of readers. Younger teens are faced with so many first experiences of becoming an adult. How they react and adapt to these changes can make a big difference in who they later become. The resources in this list will help them figure out this changing time.

Everything Is Changing!

Bailey, Jacqui. **Sex, Puberty and All that Stuff: A Guide to Growing Up.** New York: Barron's, 2004.

Through cartoons and teen language, the author aims to demystify the changes that occur during the teen years. Bailey outlines the bodily and hormonal aspects of puberty and exposes myths such as the perils of too much masturbation. Also covered are same-sex attraction, managing a good relationship, and contraception.

Crump, Marguerite. **Don't Sweat It!: Every Body's Answers to Questions You Don't Want to Ask.** Minneapolis, MN: Free Spirit, 2002.

This frank, reassuring, humorous book covers the physical changes boys and girls experience during puberty, and offers tips on caring for oneself from head to toe. Especially written for younger teens and upper elementary school students.

Deak, Erzsi, and Kristin Litchman. **Period Pieces: Stories for Girls.** New York: HarperCollins, 2003.

Suggested for girls in grades four through seven, this is a collection of twelve stories about girls' experiences as they begin to menstruate. There is no mention of sex, and the stories do not get into the purposes behind having a period for those who are not ready to learn about these aspects yet.

Dee, Catherine. **The Girls' Guide to Life: Take Charge of Your Personal Life, Your School Time, Your Social Scene, and Much More!** New York: Little, Brown, 2005.

This self-help book focuses on relationships, careers, politics, sports, and more. With a target audience of nine through fifteen-year-olds, the author gives an historical background on the feminist movement.

Dickerson, Karle. **On the Spot: Real Girls on Periods, Growing Up, and Finding Your Groove.** Avon, MA: Adams Media Corporation, 2004.

From PMS to first bras to fluctuating feelings, this sassy yet safe book for the'tween market by a writer for *Teen Magazine* reaches out to girls in their own words, helping them to understand the changes their bodies are going through.

Editors of *Girls' Life*. **The Girls' Life Guide to Growing Up.** Hillsboro, OR: Beyond Words, 2000.

The editors of the magazine *Girls' Life* present their best advice from five years of their popular magazine in one hip, honest, and street-smart guide to growing up.

Holyoke, Nancy. **A Smart Girl's Guide to Boys: Surviving Crushes, Staying True to Yourself, & Other Stuff.** With illustrations by Bonnie Timmons. Middleton, WI: American Girl Library, 2001.

This insightful, age-appropriate guide is filled with tips on being friends, going out, getting dumped, and more. A very comprehensive resource with a detailed table of contents for quick referral to several of the key topics younger teens may want to read and learn about.

Kaplowitz, Paul. **Early Puberty in Girls: An Essential Guide to Coping with This Common Problem.** New York: Ballatine Books, 2003.

A pediatric endocrinologist provides information about this more frequent occurrence of early puberty in girls, especially in African American adolescent girls.

Kirberger, Kimberley, ed. **No Body's Perfect: Stories by Teens about Body Image, Self Acceptance, and the Search for Identity.** New York: Scholastic, 2003.

A collection of stories, essays, and poetry written for teens by teens. Topics cover body image, self-identification, and self-worth. You may recognize this author's name as she coauthored *Chicken Soup for the Teenage Soul* and offers her advice and inspiration through public speaking engagements.

Le Jeune, Veronique. **Feeling Freakish?: How to Be Comfortable in Your Own Skin.** New York: Harry M. Abrams, 2004.

Describes the changes that occur during puberty and encourages young people to be less self-critical and to accept, be patient with, and care for their changing bodies.

Loulan, JoAnn. **Period: A Girl's Guide to Menstruation with a Parent's Guide.** Minnetonka, MN: Book Peddlers, 2001.

This book discusses the physical and psychological changes at the onset of menstruation. It also includes a guide for parents and teachers. This book is also distributed in Spanish.

Madaras, Lynda. **Ready Set Grow: A What's Happening to My Body? Guide for Younger Girls.** New York: Newmarket Press, 2003.

This book discusses changes in girls' bodies.

Madaras, Lynda. **The What's Happening to My Body?: Book for Boys; a Growing-Up Guide for Parents and Sons.** New York: New Market Press, 2000.

In this republished version, the author omits chapters from previous versions about sex and birth control. This newer version was adapted to fit a younger audience, since youth are learning much earlier about these issues. The chapters discuss changes that take place in a boy's body during puberty, including information on the body's changing size and shape, the growth spurt, reproductive organs, pubic hair, beards, pimples, voice changes, wet dreams, and puberty in girls.

Madaras, Lynda. **The What's Happening to My Body?: Book for Girls; a Growing-Up Guide for Parents and Daughters.** New York: New Market Press, 2000.

Selected as a "Best Book for Young Adults" by the Young Adult Library Services Association, a division of the American Library Association, this is the classic puberty education book for girls ages eight through fifteen. It is now thoroughly updated and freshly redesigned for the first time in twelve years. In age-appropriate language, the book covers the body's changing size and shape, breasts, the reproductive organs, the menstrual cycle, pubic hair, puberty in boys, diet, exercise, and health, with help on avoiding weight problems and eating disorders. Internet resources and much more are provided.

McCoy, Kathy. **Growing and Changing: A Handbook for Preteens.** New York: Berkley Publishing Group, 2003.

Addresses questions preteens have about puberty in such areas as body changes, changes in feelings, hygiene, health problems, and talking to doctors and parents.

Mosatche, Harriet S. **Too Old for This, Too Young for That!: Your Survival Guide for the Middle-School Years.** Minneapolis, MN: Free Spirit, 2000.

This book features quizzes, stories, surveys, and activities for middle schoolers, addressing such issues as physical and emotional changes, connecting with friends and family, setting goals, and handling peer pressure.

Pascoe, Elaine, ed. **Teen Dreams: A Journey through Puberty.** San Diego, CA: Blackbirch Press, 2004.

Working with The Learning Channel, Blackbirch has created this unique series about the inner workings of the human body. Incredible, cutting-edge computer graphics take you on journeys inside the body and show you step by step, on a micro level, how the body reacts to viruses, bacteria, pregnancy, puberty, poisoning, and much more. Each book focuses on personal stories of human subjects and relates what is happening inside their bodies to how they react outside. Each story focuses on what the subject has experienced. This might help the reader understand that all people are not always alike, or they may discover that they have experienced something similar.

Pleasant Company. **Yikes!: A Smart Girl's Guide to Surviving Tricky, Sticky, Icky Situations.** Middleton, WI: Pleasant Company Publication, 2002.

Provides strategies for dealing with embarrassing, emotional, or frightening situations, including forgetting your lines on stage, being threatened by a bully, or losing your parents in a big city.

Potash, Marlin S. **Am I Weird Or Is This Normal? Advice and Info To Get Teens in the Know.** New York: Simon & Schuster, 2001.

Funny and irreverent, a psychologist mom and her teenage daughter provide girls with substantive answers to their most important questions about adolescence, from sex and relationships to school, parents, and developing personal standards.

Shaffer, Susan Morris. **Why Boys Don't Talk and Why it Matters: A Parent's Survival Guide to Connecting with Your Teen.** New York: McGraw-Hill, 2005.

Unfortunately, there are many more books geared toward young girls than toward young boys when it comes to the 'tween and teen years. This is an example of a book written for the parents and caretakers of young boys. The book includes tips on how to connect when they are pushing you away, fostering closeness, working with or parenting adolescent boys of different cultural backgrounds, and breaking the masculinity myth.

Sonna, Linda. **The Everything Tween Book: A Parent's Guide to Surviving the Turbulent Preteen Years.** Avon, MA: Adams Media Corporation, 2003.

The "'tween" years, which fall between the ages of eight and twelve, can often be a challenging time for both parents and children. Child psychologist Sonna helps parents navigate the trying years and cope with a child's psychological, social, and emotional needs.

Religion, the Sometimes Dreaded 200s

If you are a school librarian, you know how controversial religious material can be in your collection. You work to make sure that the titles you order are aligned with the curriculum and needs of your students and staff. If you are a public librarian you want to ensure that the resources you provide are representative of anyone who might walk in looking for religious and spiritual information from your community. Regardless of the seriousness of this topic it is truly popular with many teens. Many have been raised to practice a specific religion and are looking to strengthen their knowledge, or they may be looking to other religions for answers. Younger teens may also be looking to discover their spiritual side for the first time. Here are a few appropriate resources for younger teens. Again, I have made an effort to provide a variety of approaches to meet differing needs. If you are looking to clarify information on religion in public schools or the public sector, consult http://www.adl.org/religion_ps_2004/ or http://www.teachingaboutreligion.org/ for further legal details.

Abadie, M. J. **The Goddess in Every Girl: Develop Your Teen Feminine Power.** Rochester, VT: Bindu Books, 2002.
> The author of *Love Planets* and *Teen Astrology* now teaches teen girls to get in touch with their own personal Goddess energy and allies.

Breully, Elizabeth, Joanne OBrien, and Martin Palmer. **Religions of the World: The Illustrated Guide to Origins, Beliefs, Traditions and Festivals, rev. ed.** New York: Facts On File, 2005.
> Outlines the beliefs and practices of major religions such as Judaism, Christianity, Islam, Hinduism, Buddhism, Jainism, Shintoism, Taoism, Sikhism, and Baha'i. The photos and diagrams show typical worship, maps, calendars, and symbols, and the information on the various religions covers scriptures from the different texts used, as well as major updates and divisions within the various religions.

Byrd, Sandra. **Stuff 2 Do: A-to-Z Activities for Girls Like You.** Minneapolis, MN: Bethany House, 2000.
> This book offers solutions for rainy days, as well as fun party themes, craft projects, and more. Many of the suggestions came from young readers all over the country. These activities are woven together with ways to become closer to God.

Feinstein, Edward. **Tough Questions Jews Ask: A Young Adult's Guide to Building a Jewish Life.** New York: Jewish Lights Publishing, 2004.
> Focuses on Jewish history and theology, written by a rabbi.

Ford, Michael Thomas. **Paths of Faith: Conversations about Religion and Spirituality.** New York: Simon & Schuster, 2000.
> In a series of revealing interviews, several prominent religious figures discuss the tenets and traditions of their religions, and focus on the personal side, sharing how they came to their religious beliefs, the issues they have struggled with, and the challenges they have faced. Each interview is prefaced with an overview of the religion.

Kise, Jane. **Find Your Fit: Dare to Act on Who You Are.** Minneapolis, MN: Bethany House, 2000.
> Developed by professionals in Christian youth ministry and personality testing, this book helps teens discover their uniqueness relating to their talents, personality types, skills, passions, and Christian values.

Smith, Christian, and Melinda Lundquist Denton. **Soul Searching: The Religious and Spiritual Lives of American Teenagers.** London: Oxford University Press, 2005.

In most discussions and analyses of American teenage life, one major topic is often overlooked—religion. However, American teens say religious faith is important in their lives. What is going on in their religious and spiritual lives? What do they actually believe? What religious practices do they engage in? Do they expect to remain loyal to the faith of their parents, or are they abandoning traditional religious institutions in search of a new, more "authentic," spirituality? Answering these and many other questions, *Soul Searching* tells the story of the religious and spiritual lives of contemporary American teenagers.

Dealing with Friends and Family

As younger teens begin to grow older, they naturally begin to pull away from one of these groups in order to form tighter bonds with the other. Can you guess which one? Of course you know that their friends are becoming increasingly more like their family. They are establishing their independence from family but will then bounce back in a sporadic way. Here are some helpful suggestions to put on your shelf during this transition.

Cadier, Florence. **My Parents Are Getting Divorced: How to Keep It Together When Your Mom and Dad Are Splitting Up.** New York: Amulet Books, 2004.

This book explains the feelings and questions shared by young adults whose parents are getting divorced, the changes that could occur, and how to deal with them. It includes hotline numbers and is specifically suggested for grades five through eight.

Criswell, Patti Kelley. **A Smart Girl's Guide to Friendship Troubles: Dealing with Fights, Being Left Out and the Whole Popularity Thing.** Middleton, WI: Pleasant Company, 2003.

From backstabbing to bullying to just being left out, here is advice for girls on a whole host of friendship problems. The book contains tips and quizzes. Real-life stories about girls who have solved their friendship problems round out this timely advice book.

Prima Girls. **Talking about Friends: Real-Life Advice from Girls like You.** Roseville, CA: Prima Girls, 2001.

Talking about Friends helps readers deal with topics including changing friendships, boys, gossip, and how to be a better friend.

Shaw, Victoria. **Best Buds: A Girl's Guide to Friendship.** New York: Rosen Publishing, 2004.

Best Buds describes the importance of friendships among preteen and teenage girls, offering advice on choosing friends and getting along with them.

Somers, Michael A. **Chillin': A Guy's Guide to Friendship.** New York: Rosen Publishing, 2000.

    This resource provides advice on making new friends and negotiating issues such as peer pressure, acceptance, and conformity.

Earning Money and Volunteering

Along with the greater independence mentioned above comes the need to be more financially free, and hopefully philanthropic as well. I have combined these two subjects together with possible resources to assist young teens.

Beyond Words Publishing. **Teen Dream Jobs: How to Find the Job You Really Want Now!** Hillsboro, OR: Beyond Words Publishing, 2003.

    Many preteens and teens fantasize about having a cool, fun job that pays. What most do not know is that it is possible for them to start pursuing their dream career right now. This is the complete guide for kids and teens who want to find their ideal job. Chapters include "What's Your Passion?—Discovering Your Dream Job," "Help Wanted? Where to Look for Your Dream Job," and "It's All about You!"

Karnes, Frances, and Kristen Stephens. **Empowered Girls: A Girl's Guide to Positive Activism, Volunteering and Philanthropy.** Austin, TX: Prufrock Press, 2005.

    A collection of empowering volunteer stories designed to motivate and inspire readers to get involved and inspire others to make a difference and change lives with projects in their school and community.

Kiyosaki, Robert T. **Rich Dad Poor Dad for Teens: The Secrets about Money That You Don't Learn in School!** New York: Warner Business Books, 2004.

    This just-for-teens edition builds a foundation of self-confidence from which readers can realize their dreams of financial security in an increasingly challenging and unreliable job market. Teen-friendly advice, examples, sidebars, and straight talk will supplement all of *Rich Dad's* core advice: Work to learn, not to earn. Don't say "I can't afford it." Instead, say "How can I afford it?" And don't work for money—make money work for you! This would be a resource for a younger teen already interested in making money and showing signs of young entrepreneurship.

Murkoff, Heidi. **The What to Expect Baby-Sitter's Handbook.** New York: Workman, 2003.

    This book is like a miniature reference tool for any babysitter. Readers can gather developmental information about children, or flip through topics and emergency information quickly. There is also a question and answer section highlighting the sixty most frequently asked questions by babysitters.

Olsen, Timothy. **The Teenage Investor: How to Start Early, Invest Often, and Build Wealth.** New York: McGraw-Hill, 2003.

> With a diverse portfolio in hand, a thirteen-year-old "wonder kid" explains to teens how to build wealth in the stock market by starting now. His fresh perspective makes *The Teenage Investor* a welcome relief from the standard "how to get rich" investment book.

Wandberg, Robert. **Volunteering: Giving Back.** Mankato, MI: Capstone Press, 2001.

> Shows many ways teens can volunteer in order to give off themselves. This resource includes information on volunteering as well as different areas of volunteerism, such as hospitals, hotlines, the environment, and blood or organ donation. Describes practical tips to get started with volunteering.

Academic and Personal Success

Not too long ago, I had a young lady burst out in tears because I had given the group she was in a task during their library media time and she was not able to finish. We quickly worked through her frustration and I consoled her on the task. There will always be young adolescents who strive for perfection, and then there are the other ones! My point is that they all need encouragement and guidance no matter what their goals. I have included books here to meet the varying needs of young patrons.

Asgedom, Mawi. **The Code: The 5 Secrets of Teen Success.** New York: Little, Brown, 2003.

> Offers advice for teens on how to succeed in school and beyond. Having overcome enormous obstacles himself during a childhood in war-torn Africa, the author is now a successful motivational speaker, and addresses teens in a straightforward no-nonsense way with advice ("Give first, receive second," is secret #3), personal experiences, and motivational exercises.

Bachel, Beverly K. **What Do You Really Want? How to Set a Goal and Go for It!: A Guide for Teens.** Minneapolis, MN: Free Spirit, 2001.

> A motivational book aimed at teenagers that provides tips on setting goals and achieving them, as well as exercises and reproducible forms to help track one's progress.

Carlson, Richard. **Don't Sweat the Small Stuff for Teens: Simple Ways to Keep Your Cool in Stressful Times.** New York: Hyperion, 2000.

> Teens and their parents will learn how not to stress out about homework, peer pressure, dating, and other potentially difficult areas.

Carroll, Jamuna. **Students Rights: Opposing Viewpoints.** Detroit, MI: Greenhaven Press/Thomson Gale, 2005.

A think-tank resource that offers opinions from both sides of an issue. Issues covered in this book relate to students rights regarding their quality of education, personal expression, and privacy.

Cordes, Helen. **Girl Power in the Classroom: A Book about Girls, Their Fears, and Their Future.** Minneapolis, MN: Lerner Publications, 2000.

This book discusses the particular challenges, expectations, and stereotypes girls face in the classroom. Each book in this series talks with girls and the people who care about them in order to provide new insights into growing up.

Erlbach, Arlene. **The Middle School Survival Guide.** New York: Walker, 2003.

This guidebook was designed to help preteens deal with changes in school, families, social lives, and bodies that come during the middle school years, with specific advice for a variety of situations.

Esperald, Pamela. **Life Lists for Teens: Tips, Steps, Hints, and How-tos for Growing Up, Getting Along, Learning and Having Fun.** Minneapolis, MN: Free Spirit, 2003.

Hundreds of lists provide guidance in areas of young adult life, as diverse as selecting a book or a hair color to choosing a mentor.

Espeland, Pamela. **Succeed Every Day: Daily Reading for Teens.** Minneapolis, MN: Free Spirit, 2000.

Topics such as friendship, courage, achievement, spirituality, and family are covered in this guide to daily living for teens.

Packer, Alex J. **Highs!: Over 150 Ways to Feel Really, Really Good Without Alcohol or Other Drugs**. Minneapolis, MN: Free Spirit, 2000.

With his trademark wit and style, Packer describes more than 150 safe, creative, and natural ways to find contentment, pleasure, excitement, insight, or peace, without the use of alcohol or drugs. He explains the benefits of breathing and meditation exercises, physical exercise, food, creativity, family, friends, and more.

Packer, Alex. **The How Rude! Handbook of School Manners for Teens: Civility in the Hallowed Halls.** Minneapolis, MN: Free Spirit, 2004.

Here is sound advice (touched with humor) for teens who want to make their school lives more bearable. *The How Rude! Handbook* answers questions such as what to do when someone wants to copy from your homework, or what to do when a teacher is rude, and more.

Mosatche, Harriet S. **Too Old for This, Too Young for That!: Your Survival Guide for the Middle-School Years.** Minneapolis, MN: Free Spirit, 2000.

This book provides quizzes, stories, surveys, and activities for middle schoolers, addressing such issues as physical and emotional changes, connecting with friends and family, setting goals, and handling peer pressure.

Personal Style

Picture this: a young, beautiful girl of yesterday with long, flowing brown hair suddenly walks into the library with streaks of pink or purple and funky jewelry. Or is this the young man you swear was just hugging you after story time and is now barely talking to you unless he truly cannot find what he is looking for? You hardly recognize him under the brim of his twisted baseball cap and baggy pants, which now allow you to see his brand of underwear! Those in early adolescence are beginning to establish their own personal style through a variety of ways and outlets. And just as we would look for the latest height in fall fashion boots or skirts, younger teens begin to work toward establishing their own style and identifying who they are and want to be.

Jaynes, Ela. **Planet Yumthing Do-It-Yourself: Create, Design, Reinvent, and Make It Yours!** New York: Bantam Books, 2004.

> These cool, easy, and hip fashion accessory and home decor projects give readers the chance to show off their individuality, and no sewing machine is required! Easy-to-follow steps guide readers through each project, and sweet and sassy illustrations make the process extra fun. Whether it is fashion, beauty, decor, or food and friends, this book will give you tons of original projects that are not only easy (really!) to do, but also well within your budget.

Muharrar, Aisha. **More than a Label: Why What You Wear and Who You're With Doesn't Define Who You Are.** Minneapolis, MN: Free Spirit, 2002.

> Drawn from a survey of more than one thousand teenagers. First-person stories help to address the problems inherent in labeling people.

O'Sullivan, Joanne. **Girls' World: Making Cool Stuff for Your Room, Your Friends & You.** New York: Lark Books, 2002.

> A collection of dozens of ideas and step-by-step instructions for decorating a bedroom, school supplies, and locker; as well as creating cosmetics, clothing, and accessories that express one's personal style.

Pleasant Company. **Room for You: Find Your Style and Make Your Room Say You!** Middleton, WI: Pleasant Company Publications, 2001.

> Includes a quiz to help readers discover their decorating style and gives them ideas for rooms. Includes tips on sharing a room and cleaning.

Smith, Allison Chandler. **The Girl's World Book of Bath & Beauty: Fresh Ideas & Fun Recipes for Hair, Skin, Nails & More.** New York: Lark Books, 2004.

> Describes how to make moisturizers, bath salts, scrubs, lip glosses, and shampoos using natural ingredients from health food stores and other easily found supplies.

Hobbies and Interests

As a young teen, I had a fascination with my hopeful future as a legally driving citizen! I would save catalog pictures of cars I hoped to someday own. And oh, the memories of watching "Can't Buy Me Love" (1987) and admiring Cyndi as she drove around in her white Volkswagon Cabriolet Convertible. I just knew I would someday have this type of car that would surely help me gain popularity and status as a high school driver. Many younger teens have hobbies and interests that show their future interests as older teens and adults, yet still embrace their hobbies of yesterday. After all, I finally got my convertible but it was many years later when I could actually afford to purchase one myself. Here are a few books that represent information needs for today's younger teens.

Case, Barbara. **Making Beaded Jewelry: Over 80 Beautiful Designs to Make and Wear.** United Kingdom: David & Charles, 2003.

> Learn how to make a wide range of gorgeous beads, from antique to exotic, into fashionable and original jewelry.

Dahlstrom, Lorraine M. **Writing Down the Days: 365 Creative Journaling Ideas for Young People.** Minneapolis, MN: Free Spirit, 2000.

> This collection contains over 300 journal activities for beginning writers and over 1,000 other activities for teachers to introduce in the classroom, including puzzles, books to read, contests, and crafts.

Haney, Eric L. **Inside Delta Force: The Story of America's Elite Counterterrorist Unit.** New York: Delacorte, 2006.

> The author, a retired commander sergeant major and an Army ranger, describes the Delta Force unit at Fort Bragg.

Maurer, Tracy. **Cheerleading Skills.** Vero Beach, FL: Rourke Publishing, 2006.

> This is only one of the titles from a new series *Jump and Shout*. This book is recommended for reluctant readers because of its high interest and lower reading level. Cheerleading has continuously been a hot topic with younger teens, and if this is a hobby of the teens you serve, it might be a hit with personal interests and hobbies.

Miller, Steve. **Freaks! How to Draw Fantastic Fantasy Creatures.** New York: Watson- Guptill, 2004.

> *Freaks* provides step-by-step instructions for creatively drawing a variety of fantasy creatures, including werewolves, unicorns, insect people, feathered creatures, and more.

Ozawa, Tadashi. **How to Draw Anime and Game Characters.** Japan: Graphic-sha, 2003.

This series is now up to volume four and includes techniques in several different areas of anime. Sure to never be on your shelf for more than a day!

Winters, Adam. **Everything You Need to Know about Being a Teen Driver.** New York: Rosen, 2000.

The reader will learn about becoming a licensed driver and such related concerns as getting your first car, road safety, drinking and driving, and road rage. Although many younger teens are not ready to start the driving process, others like me just want to find out as much as they can so they can dabble in the world of being older than they actually are.

Looking Good, Staying Fit

Bartell, Susan S. **Dr. Susan's Girls-Only Weight Loss Guide: The Easy, Fun Way to Look Good.** New York: Parent Positive Press, 2006.

Includes quizzes and advice on developing a healthy lifestyle and tackling problems that lead to obesity, such as peer pressure, genetics, and puberty.

Gaede, Katrina. **Fitness Training for Girls: A Teen Girl's Guide to Resistance Training, Cardiovascular Conditioning and Nutrition.** San Diego, CA: Tracks Publishing, 2001.

Eleven chapters describe the importance of fitness for women and girls, from goal setting, using facilities, and stretching, to cardio and strength-training exercises and eating habits. The recommended exercises are explained and illustrated with black-and-white drawings and photographs. The visuals and charts list exercises for different body parts and for basketball, cross-country, golf, softball, tennis, track and field, and other sports that can be used by beginners or trainees. The list of resources includes books, magazines, organizations, and Web sites that will appeal to this audience.

Platkin, Charles Stuart. **Lighten Up: Stay Sane, Eat Great, Lose Weight.** New York: Razorbill, 2005.

This resource shares ideas on how teens can eat healthy and light no matter where they are. Younger teens will find out how to have willpower and make smart trade-offs in order to fulfill their cravings yet satisfy their need to stay healthy.

Sanna, Ellyn. **America's Unhealthy Lifestyle: Supersize It!** Philadelphia, PA: Mason Crest Publishers, 2006.

This book examines the American epidemic of overeating and examines how this is creating a population that is not only obese but very unhealthy as well.

Steinfeld, Jake. **Get Strong! Body by Jake's Guide to Building Confidence, Muscles, and a Great Future for Teenage Guys.** New York: Fireside, 2002.

This whole approach to fitness, physical fitness via mental strength, inspires teenage guys to set goals for themselves. Jake includes dozens of stories about guys who started making progress only after setting goals.

Vedral, Joyce L. **Toning for Teens: The 20-Minute Workout That Makes You Look Good and Feel Great!** New York: Warner Books, 2002.

In a total body weight training book for teens, fitness expert Vedral teaches girls how to use weights to build strong, physically fit bodies, and coaches girls through diet and weight training workouts.

Incredible but True Stories

Many younger adolescents like to read about others their age and how they made a difference or impacted others through their talents, triumphs or tragedies. The following is a list of short story collections of real-life experiences of young people from the past and present.

Atkin, S. Beth, ed. **Gun Stories: Life-Changing Experiences with Guns.** New York: Katherine Tegen Books/HarperCollins, 2006.

This is a chronicle of thirty-four school shootings that occurred between 1995 and 2005, focusing on people who were affected by the shootings. There are also stories about gun-related problems with drive-bys, accidental shootings, and suicide.

Bartoletti, Susan Campbell. **Hitler Youth.** New York: Scholastic Nonfiction, 2005.

This was a 2006 Newbery honor book about the zeal of the youth under Adolf Hitler from 1933 to 1945. A direct and dangerous example of how such young growing minds can believe and process misinformation and persuasion.

Canfield, Jack, Mark Victor Hansen, Patty Hansen, Irene Dunlap, and Rusty Fischer. **Chicken Soup for the Preteen Soul: 101 Stories of Changes, Choices, and Growing Up for Kids Ages 9 to 13.** Deerfield Beach, FL: Health Communications, 2000.

This survival guide to the preteen years is packed with stories by and about readers ages ten to thirteen. This uplifting collection touches on the emotions and situations preteens experience every day: making and losing friends, fitting in while keeping a personal identity, discovering the opposite sex, dealing with pressures at school, and coping with family issues. Includes stories by *NSYNC, Mia Hamm, Beverly Mitchell, and Karl Malone.

McCann, Michelle Roehm. **Girls Who Rocked the World 2: Heroines from Harriet Tubman to Mia Hamm.** Hillsboro, OR: Beyond Words, 2000.

Profiles young women from around the world who accomplished great things while still teenagers, including Harriet Tubman, Florence Nightingale, and Mia Hamm, and presents writings from modern American girls describing how they plan to "rock the world."

Morris, Deborah. **Teens 911: Snowbound.** Deerfield Beach, FL: Health Communications, 2002.

A new reality series of chilling true-life dramas. Three Washington teenagers face hypothermia on a ski trip gone wrong. The thirteen-year-old daughter of a Texas cop uses skills she has learned from him to respond when his experimental helicopter crashes. A New York teen saves his younger brother and sister from a deadly fire. A rodeo competitor in New Mexico uses CPR skills when she finds a teacher in full cardiac arrest. Two brothers from Idaho join forces to rescue their father after he is badly injured on a rafting trip. The book is full of excitement about teens, which can truly empower the reader.

ELECTRONIC MATERIALS

When it comes to retrieving information for research projects or for general information needs, younger teens are typically aware of basic searching strategies on the Internet. They may "google" their way to a Web site containing information about their topic. Often times they are not information literate when it comes to evaluating these sources and knowing what is available to them. Adults often assume that teens are very savvy on the Web, and for the most part they are more aware of its features. Our job as librarians is to make sure they know what their options are and encourage them to be selective about where the information is coming from. Younger adolescents may also know that the library has software, but I often find they are not aware of the databases available to them with their library card. Having electronic databases at your library is a wonderful way to provide on-site and remote access to electronic information for multiple customers.

Appleman, Daniel. **Always Use Protection: A Teen's Guide to Safe Computing.** Berkeley, CA: Apress, 2004.

A helpful resource for younger teens looking to equip themselves with protection in the area of computer security and online safety. The author provides the information teens, or anyone else for that matter, should have before venturing out onto the Internet.

ELECTRONIC COMMUNICATION

Chat Rooms

Let us face it, teens are chatting with others online. Whether you agree or disagree with this form of communication, it is important to offer some reliable information for younger teens. There has been a lot of negative publicity and even books written about the dangers of communicating via the Web: young teens can become easy prey to criminals on the Web as illustrated in *Katie.com: My Story*. In this book, a young teen becomes the first victim to successfully prosecute a pedophile via the new Internet laws. Teens need to know that they cannot give out personal information on the Web, and efforts have been made to make sure that parents and teens are more aware of safety concerns on the Web. Sites like www.chatdanger.com are produced by organizations like Childnet International that work toward making the Internet a safer place for youth. Teaching our youth how to interact responsibly when chatting or instant messaging is no different than asking them to be safe and responsible when they leave the house. However, we must ourselves be knowledgeable of the resources in order to prepare them before they enter this new arena of communication. According to a recent article by Linda Braun, this type of online communication is second only to e-mail communication. According to her, "Librarians must learn those techniques so they can help teens use them" (Braun 2005).

Kidz World.com. Kidz World Media. Accessed January 15, 2005, available at http://www.kidzworld.com/chat/
   A Web site that offers good choices to kids who want to chat or post messages on message boards.

YA Authors Café. YA Authors Café: Good Books, Good Friends, Good Chat . . . Welcome. Accessed May 2, 2005, available at http://ourworld .cs.com/YAAuthorsCafe/
   Authors and their fans are able to talk about their books and discuss them through this chat forum.

Electronic Lists

Electronic lists are something you may participate in at your current work setting, but this is also a way by which teens can gain information about some of their favorite topics. As librarians, I think we need to ensure that they know the information may not always be accurate depending on the type of list they subscribe to. Some of the main differences occur because, while the host of some mailing lists may browse the information before sending it out, other types are not monitored before the information is sent out to those on the list. Make sure that the list you suggest they sign up for is age appropriate and is hosted by someone reliable and trustworthy. There are so many out there. To find a good one you simply need to use your selection criteria for other materials in the Web site section and apply it to information mailing lists.

Database Subscriptions

Database subscriptions are a great way to provide information to all customers, and teens are especially fond of their electronic format. The biggest battle with databases and younger teens is creating adequate publicity for the resource, and making sure that the teens know how to use and how to cite the resource. Many patrons, including teens, are confused when accessing databases. They may assume that it is just another Web site or claim that they have already searched the Web and did not find anything. I often go and pull a magazine from the shelf on the wall, bring it over to the computer, and explain that this is something we subscribe to on the Web and that you are simply accessing it on the Web rather than flipping through the pages. It is also helpful to have style guides available, or more specific information pulled out, or even a link created on how to cite electronic resources. As we all know, it can be quite confusing.

Most databases allow a free trial subscription enabling you to make sure the resource will be a good match for the users in your community. It is a good idea to keep abreast of the new databases appropriate for younger teens. You can often learn about these through colleagues via professional mailing lists or library/information technology conferences. Get an idea of the databases that are popular by browsing comparable library Web sites for what they offer. Take a look at the library demographics for a similar community sample. Once you have found some that you are interested in, contact the database company, or visit their Web site for free trial subscription information. This can be just for you to explore, or they may offer free licensing for your young customers as well. This allows you to ask their opinion of the database before purchasing.

Facts on File News Services

This is part of the WRC Media family. The Facts for Learning Middle School module provides core reference content for middle school students of all levels. The more sophisticated interface and subject matter respect their abilities, but still deliver content written for students in grades five through eight.

WRC Media. New York: Facts on File for Learning. **Facts on File News Services.** Retrieved August 15, 2004, available at http://www.facts.com/index.htm.

Grolier Online

The Grolier Online product is actually made up of seven databases: Encyclopedia Americana, Grolier Multimedia Encyclopedia, New Book of

Knowledge, La Nueva Encyclopedia Cumbre, The New Book of Popular Science, Lands and People, and America the Beautiful. It provides a wealth of information ranging from generalized resources to category specific databases depending on the teen's need. Search all databases at once or go specifically to one in order to locate your information. A free thirty-day trial is available for this product.

Scholastic Library Publishing. New York: Grolier Online. Retrieved February 10, 2006, available at http://www.go.grolier.com.

ProQuest Learning: Literature

ProQuest Learning: Literature delivers more than 180,000 searchable works of literature from medieval times to the present. Students can find author biographies, contemporary criticism, reviews, and multimedia resources organized into over 3,000 Author Pages. It also features over forty searchable full-text literary journals and magazines for the latest in literary criticism.

ProQuest. Ann Arbor, MI: ProQuest Information and Learning Company. Retrieved December 27, 2004, available at http://www.proquestk12.com/pic/literature.shtml.

Literature Resource Center 3.0

With the Literature Resource Center 3.0, you can provide students and other researchers with single-search access to an assortment of traditional literary reference works, critical information on authors and their works, current journal articles, and additional resources in an easy-to-use interface that utilizes the powerful yet simple searchability of the Internet.

Thomas Gale. Farmington Hills, MI: Opposing Viewpoints Resource Center. Retrieved July 24, 2004, available at http://www.gale.com/OpposingView points/index.htm.

Opposing Viewpoints Resource Center

The Opposing Viewpoints Resource Center database draws on the acclaimed social issues series published by Greenhaven Press, as well as core reference content from other Gale and Macmillan Reference USA sources to provide a complete one-stop source for information on social issues. You can access viewpoint articles, topic overviews, statistics, primary documents, links to Web sites, and full-text magazine and newspaper articles. Also offered is a research guide, which will help young students with their process of critical thinking, analyzing current topics and citing their sources.

Thomas Gale. Farmington Hills, MI: Opposing Viewpoints Resource Center. Retrieved July 24, 2004, available at http://www.gale.com/OpposingView points/index.htm.

The Student Resource Center 3.0

A fully integrated database containing thousands of curriculum-targeted primary documents, biographies, topical essays, background information, critical analyses, full-text coverage of 200 magazines, over 10,000 photographs and illustrations, and more than eight hours of audio and video clips.

Thomas Gale. Farmington Hills, MI: Student Resource Center. Retrieved July 24, 2004, available at http://www.galegroup.com/SRC/.

SIRS Knowledge Source

SIRS Knowledge Source is a complete database that comprises several distinct reference databases including SIRS Researcher®, SIRS Government Reporter®, SIRS Renaissance®, SKS WebSelect™, SIRS Discoverer®, and Discoverer WebFind™. Updated daily, the database provides relevant, credible information on social issues, science, history, government, the arts, and humanities. The featured full-text articles and Internet resources are carefully chosen from thousands of domestic and international publications and respected organizations. This resource also has a librarian's corner, which includes citing information and lesson ideas for teachers and librarians. Educators may find it helpful to use the links to state and national learning standards.

ProQuest. Ann Arbor, MI: ProQuest Information and Learning Company.Retrieved December 27, 2004, available at http://www.proquestk12.com/pic/knowledge.shtml.

ProQuest History Study Center

History Study Center is an online resource that offers students digitized primary and secondary sources. Database users are able to find past journal articles, rare books, newspaper articles, video clips, parliamentary papers, criminal trial records, radio and television news, maps, images, student guides, and a bookshelf of prominent reference titles. Also featured is a History Web Gateway, which provides links to thousands of reliable and informative Web sites. History Study Center offers over 40,000 documents and articles from hundreds of widely studied topics, with over 50 reference works, 3,000 images, and links to 2,000 Web sites.

ProQuest. Ann Arbor, MI: ProQuest Information and Learning Company. History Study Center. Retrieved December 27, 2004, http://www .proquestk12.com/pic/study.shtml.

ONLINE REFERENCE AND TUTORIAL SERVICES

Many libraries today provide online reference services that are either local or cooperative with other librarians in the region or state. This type of online chat service typically allows live interaction with a librarian twenty-four hours a day, seven days a week. This is especially beneficial to younger adolescents who may have sports practice or other after-school activities, then come home to dinner and only get around to their homework after the public library is already closed. Younger adolescents are typically quite comfortable with this type of communication via the computer. In fact, they might actually prefer this type of assistance to a face-to-face interaction with a librarian, especially if the librarian is not very youth friendly. Make sure that younger teens are aware of these services and provide information on how they work.

Ask Us Now 24/7 Reference Service

This product is specific to residents and public library users of certain states such as Maryland and Delaware. There are similar reference service programs available in other states, however. Make sure your younger teens know about the information services available to them in your state.

Ask Us Now 24/7 Reference: A cooperative service of Maryland public libraries. Virtural Reference Desk Project. Accessed January 20, 2005, available at www.askusnow.info. Enoch Pratt Free Library & State Library Resource Center in Baltimore City.

Tutor.com Information Services

Tutor.com is an online subscription service that many libraries and schools have purchased throughout the country. You can find a list of these organizations on their Web site by state. Students are able to chat with teachers and/or librarians to access tutoring help and information services. The tutors and students have typing and drawing tools available to help with the tutoring process. All the tools can be manipulated in real time, so both parties can see the text, drawing, or Web site offered. There is also a follow up survey after each session to ensure that the student was satisfied with the tutoring experience. The student is able to print out a log of the session to keep for future reference.

Tutor.com. Accessed January 20, 2005, available at www.tutor.com.

Homework Help Online

"Homeworkhelp.com was launched in 1998, and has created a powerful tutorial site for middle and high school students, college and beyond. We make Internet a more powerful learning tool for you." Both teachers and students who want to improve their learning and lessons can use this online tool. You will need to create a login and password for this site.

Homeworkhelp.com. Accessed January 15, 2005, available at http://www .homeworkhelp.com.

COMPUTER SOFTWARE

Decisions, Decisions 5.0. (2006). Tom Snyder Productions. CD Rom Mac/ Windows.

This is the name of a series of software programs intended to allow students in grades 5–10 the opportunity to role play scenarios. Topics range from historically based scenarios to modern decision-making situations such as lying, cheating, stealing, substance abuse, and violence in America. The software also matches typical state standards in gathering and analyzing information.

YM Digital Makeover Magic. (2002). MGI Software Corporation. CD Rom Linux, Mac OS, Unix, Windows 95 / NT / Me / 2000 / 98.

Teens can create new looks, images, and fashion designs with this software. E-mail friends and change backgrounds for your picture creations.

Hollywood High. (2006). Tom Snyder Productions. CD Rom Mac/Windows.

Designed for grades 6–12, this software allows teens to write and direct plays about different situations that might reflect their own life, or be completely fictional in their storytelling. Teens are able to develop creative writing and thinking skills through the character dialog, setting(s), props, and scenes. A variety of voices and moods allow them to change each character as they wish. In the end they are able to play the whole production and evaluate their creation.

Middle School Advantage. (2005). Encore Software, a Navarre Corporation company.

The Middle School Advantage program features interactive learning activities that focus on skills in pre-algebra, algebra, reading, typing, Spanish, grammar, geometry, vocabulary, life science, and U.S. history. The program also features interactive tutors to assist students when they have questions throughout the program. Middle School Advantage is also guaranteed to help students succeed in school.

INTERNET WEB SITES

General Younger Teen Sites

Full Circle.com. Interactive Teen Websites. Accessed Janaury 20, 2005, available at http://www.fullcirc.com/teens.htm

Sponsored by Full Circle Associates, who provide a variety of online services to an array of different clients. They offer an area just for teens here that links to several helpful sites.

Awesome Library.org. Adams, Jerry. (1996). Awesome Library for Teens. Accessed January 20, 2005, available at http://www.awesomelibrary.org/student5.html

Awesome library is a great, well-organized, general reference area resource for anyone. It has a section devoted just to teens that covers several subject areas. One of the exciting features of this Web site is a new "Talk Library" download, which functions as a talking browser to enable you to have Web site text read to the user. This could be helpful to young adolescents for online books, pronunciation, and just plain fun! You can choose from a few different voices, and remember, it is free! This will be especially appealing to young adolescents. Another feature is the language selector, which allows the user to choose the language they like.

Christiananswers.net:Teen Q's. Eden Communications. (1995–2005). Teen Q's. Accessed April 29, 2005, available at www.christiananswers.net/teens

This Web site is specifically focused on answering everyday questions or concerns related to teens who are of the Christian faith and are looking for this type of perspective.

Kidshealth.org. Teens Health: Answers and Advice. Accessed January 20, 2005, available

Kidshealth.org is a well-organized and well-rounded resource for young people. They have a portion of their site dedicated just to teens. There is a large variety of topics covered and most are appropriate and handled well to meet the needs of young adolescents as well. Topics include health, jobs, volunteering, friendship, body changes, decision making, and friendship. The site also pays equal attention to both male and female issues and information.

America's Teens.gov. Moss, Vicky. (2004). *America's Teens.gov.* Accessed January 20, 2005, available at http://www.afterschool.gov/kidsnteens2.html

Sponsored by General Services Administration: The Interagency Executive Oversight Committee. This governmental site offers information to help teens do homework, pursue hobbies, choose a career, or have some fun. With an exciting look and solid links, this is a good site for younger teens looking for a large variety of information.

4 Girls Health.com. 4 Girls Health. Accessed January 20, 2005, available at http://wwws.4girls.gov/index.htm

This Web site was created especially for girls ages ten through sixteen by the National Women's Health Information Center (NWHIC), a division of the U.S. Department of Health and Human Services. This well-organized and reputable site offers younger teens and girls helpful information on their health and supportive options for healthy choices as they grow older. There are also helpful links and lessons for those of you who assist teachers with resources.

Jobs and Volunteering

Sponsored by Quintessential Careers.com, these links feature different articles about teen jobs and gives a list of do's and don'ts for teens looking to choose a teen career.

Quintessential Careers.com. (1996). Quintessential Careers. Accessed January 15, 2005, available at http://www.quintcareers.com/jobs_for_teens .html, http://www.quintcareers.com/younger_teen_job_dos-donts.html.

Employment Ideas for Young Adolescents

In Montana, "Discovering Montana" is the official Web site for the state. The site includes a helpful link highlighting different job ideas, especially for younger teens.

Discovering Montana. (1996). Workforce Services Division. Accessed January 15, 2005, available at http://jsd.dli.state.mt.us/local/missoula/youngadult/ employmentideasforyoungteens.html.

Writing

Teenlit.com. Ms. S., Dr. K. (1999). Teen Lit. Accessed January 20, 2005, available at http://www.teenlit.com

Teenlit.com was created by two secondary school teachers from Michigan. The site is supported through a grant provided by McCarthy Dressman Education Foundation. It offers some great opportunities and information for young writers.

Easybib.com: Citation Made Simple. Easy Bib. Accessed January 20, 2005, available at http://www.easybib.com

This free Web site allows users to type in the information needed to accurately compile a bibliography. You can also create a user profile to save your citations and compile them in an organized way if you are not finished in one session. This would also be a great activity to use with middle school students when covering intellectual property with students of this age. An otherwise dry subject is given a little more life when students are able to use technology to walk through the concepts. Easybib.com adheres to the MLA Style Guide and the fifth version of APA.

Hobbies

Sports Illustrated Kids.com. Sikids.com. Accessed January 20, 2005, available at http://www.sikids.com/index.html

This Web site is done in conjunction with the *Sports Illustrated for Kids* magazine. The site features information and news on most sports. There are also games, fantasy sports leagues, and chat rooms for sports enthusiasts. Although the name includes "kids," this site is still "kewl" enough for young adolescents.

Guys Read.com. Scieszka, Jon. (2005). Guys Read.com. Accessed January 20, 2005, available at http://www.guysread.com/

The mission of this site, which is backed by famous children's and young adult author Jon Scieszka, is to find ways to connect books to guys. The great thing is that he uses the word "guys" so this site is appropriate for boys and younger teens alike. The site is interactive and attractive for this audience. You can select whether you are a young, middle, or older guy and then type in a favorite author, story, or theme to connect to different books guys would like to read.

Yahoo Astrology

Yahooligans is an optional search engine with several features for kids of all ages. It also has a portion dedicated to astrology for kids. The look and interest level is a good option for younger adolescents, however.

Yahooligans Astrology. (2004). Yahooligans! Accessed January 19, 2005, available at http://yahooligans.yahoo.com/content/astrology.

Zodiac Girlz.com. The Zodiac Girlz. Available at http://www.zodiacgirlz.com.

The Zodiac Girlz site is interactive and responsibly compiled for those younger adolescents who have an interest in studying the zodiac. There is even a parent consent form and parent page that encourages parents to stay involved with the searching and online interaction of their minors.

Virtual Hairstylist. IVillage. Accessed January 2005, available at http://beauty.ivillage.com/hn/virtualhairstylist

This site allows the user to choose a face color, hair color, and a variety of colors and styles to experiment with. An adolescent girl might enjoy changing and adapting the style online before making the actual decision on herself. It is also fun to play around with as I quickly learned!

Health

An informational site project set up by the Health Information Project and funded by the New York State Office of Alcoholism and Substance Abuse Services (OASAS) and in part by Dutchess County Government Mid-Hudson Library. Teens are able to look at recommended books, movies, and Web sites from other teens and the input is regulated by the project organizers. There are aspects of the site that are more appropriate for young adolescents and other parts more appropriate for older teens. There are many sections concerning how teens can grow up healthy.

HIP-Health Information Project. (2005). Mid-Hudson Library Project. Accessed January 19, 2005, available at http://hip.midhudson.org/main.htm.

Family Doctor.org: For Teens. American Academy of Family Physicians. Available at http://familydoctor.org/teens.xml
    There is a special section dedicated to teens with advice on how to stay healthy, and common teen health conditions, sexuality, eating disorders, and dealing with drugs and alcohol.

TeensHealth.org. Teens Health. Accessed January 20, 2005, available at http://www.kidshealth.org/teen/

Safety on the Web

You can find the *Teen Safety on the Information Highway*, a publication of the National Center for Missing and Exploited Children, from http://www.safeteens.com/.

Magic, Larry. (1998). Safe Teens.com. Accessed January 20, 2005, available at http://www.safeteens.com.

CONCLUSION

Young people naturally ask questions about their environment. When they grow older, they begin the process of more abstract thinking and questioning their world. This opens up a great opportunity to ensure that they have resources available. Those in the stage of early adolescence are progressing from children to teenagers and there are many things they ponder during this time. They are also faced with social pressures to be the same as those around them. Being different is often something they fear, and younger adolescents want to make sure they are changing, developing, and maturing normally. These developing youth are able to fulfill their need to assure themselves they are okay by accessing information through a variety of sources.

No matter what the source, make sure you provide a working channel of communication with the younger teens you serve. For example, is there a developmentally appropriate way in which they can give you suggestions and feedback on the nonfiction choices you are making for them? Young adolescents have a whole world ahead of them. This is really the time when they begin to question many things in their lives, whether they be physical, philosophical, or regarding their futures. Developmentally, they have very differing needs than those in the stage of middle and late adolescence. They also have very differing needs than they had as younger children. We have the rewarding task of making sure they have appropriate information available to them and also encouraging their use and understanding of this information.

There are several things facing teens of tomorrow, technology being one of them. Young adolescents are more accepting of these different formats and are comfortable, for the most part, with different forms of media when accessing information. As librarians and media specialists, we need to make sure that the resources we provide them, once chosen, are able to be processed by the user and then be placed into any document or final form of communication.

Tomorrow's young adolescents will benefit from our choosing developmentally appropriate resources and encouraging information literacy through the use of informative resources in a variety of formats.

WORKS CITED

Blume, Judy. *Are You There God? It's Me, Margaret.* Englewood Cliffs, NJ: Bradbury Press, 1970.

Braun, Linda. "Don't Blame the Internet." *Voice of Youth Advocates* 27, no. 6 (February 2005): 467.

Can't Buy Me Love. Dir. Steve Rash. Perf. Patrick Dempsey, Amanda Peterson. Buena Vista Home Entertainment, 1987.

Carter, Betty. *Best Books for Young Adults*, 2nd ed. Chicago: American Library Association, 2000.

Chezzi, Derek. "What Your Kids Really Want." *Maclean's* 117, no. 36 (6 September, 2004): 38.

Emge, Diane. "Fat! Beating Back Unrealistic Body Images through Young Adult Literature." *Voice of Youth Advocates* 28, no. 5 (December 2005): 369–371.

Hepperman, Christine. "Laughing in the Face of Puberty." *Horn Book Magazine* 76, no. 2 (March/April 2000): 162, 7p.

Kaplan, Elaine Bell, and Leslie Cole. " 'I Want to Read Stuff on Boys': White, Lantina, and Black Girls Reading *Seventeen* Magazine and Encountering Adolescence." *Adolescence* 38, 149 (Spring 2003): 141, 19p.

Kawamoto, Dawn. Disney's MP3 Players for Teens. CNET News.com. Published September 29, 2005, available at http://news.com .com/Disneys+MP3+players+for+preteens/2100-1041_3588491 .html.

Manzo, Kathleen. "Researchers Outline Elements Needed to Achieve Adolescent Literacy." *Education Week* 24, no. 8 (20 October 2004): 10, 1p.

McNeal, James U. "It's Not Easy Being Tween." *Brandweek*, April 16, 2001. Accessed January 20, 2004, available at http://www.findarti cles.com/p/articles/mi_m0BDW/is_16_42/ai_73409575.

Shakespeare, William. *Macbeth.* New York: Washington Square Press.

Spano, Sedra. "Adolescent Brain Development." *Youth Studies Australia* 22, no. 1 (March 2003): 36, 3p.

Tarbox, Katherine. *Katie.com: My Story.* New York: Dutton, 2000.

Thompson, Steven, Michelle Weber, and Laura Beth Brown. "The Relationship between Reading Beauty and Fashion Magazines and the Use of Pathogenic Dieting Methods among Adolescent Females." *Adolescence* 37, no. 145 (Spring 2002): p1, 18p.

Todd, Ross J. "Adolescents of the Information Age: Patterns of Information Seeking and Use, and Implications for Information Professionals." *School Libraries Worldwide* 9, no. 2 (2003): 27–46.

Weinberger, David. Educational Podcasting Network. What Is a Podcast? Accessed February 17, 2006, available at http://epnweb.org/index .php?view_mode=what.

Whalen, Samuel P. *Public Libraries and Youth Development: A Guide to Practice and Policy.* Chicago, IL: Chapin Hall Center for Children at the University of Chicago, 2002.

World Book Online. *World Book Online Dictionary.* Chicago: World Book, 2006. http://www.worldbookonline.com/wb/dict?lu=blog.

Worldview Diversity. Teaching about Religion. Sacramento. Accessed February 15, 2006, available at http://www.teachingaboutreligion

.org/.Writer's Weekly. Writer's Weekly.com. Accessed January 20, 2005, available at http://www.writersweekly.com/whats_new/0011 70_01282004.html.

Young Adult Library Services Association. YALSA Professional Development Center. Chicago: American Library Association. Accessed February 11, 2006, available at http://www.ala.org/ala/yalsa/profdev/ schoolpublic.htm.

3

Fiction for 'Tweens and Young Teens

Deborah Taylor

You get to Alcatraz by being the worst of the worst. Unless you're me. I came here because my mother said I had to.—(Choldenko, Gennifer. *Al Capone Does My Shirts.* New York: G.P. Putnam, 2004.)

Many young adolescents can identify with Moose Flanagan in this Newbery Honor Award winning novel. Twelve-year-old Moose finds himself, against his wishes, a resident of Alcatraz prison because his dad takes a job as a prison warden. Younger teens are at the stage of their lives when they are still restricted by the decisions of their parents. But this does not stop them from having opinions about what happens in their lives, or, in the case of Moose, trying to find some way to make the best of the lives adults seem to control. It is also the period when young teens begin to develop the necessary skills for a successful transition to adulthood. Often, young adolescents seek and find experiences that are familiar from their own lives in the books they read for pleasure.

Young adolescents read fiction for the same reasons as others: they seek to be entertained, to enjoy a good story about interesting characters in unique or unusual circumstances. However, because young adolescents are also in a special time of personal development, reading fiction brings with it the opportunity to do more than empathize with characters: it provides an opportunity to share experiences that can add to a growing self-awareness and understanding of others.

Young adolescents are able to make these connections with characters and stories from any genre in fiction; indeed, even as young adolescents enjoy the adventures of characters in books of fantasy, it is often the developmental aspects of these characters that resonate with them. As much as young readers are thrilled by what happens to Harry Potter, they relate to the ongoing friendship and camaraderie between him and his friends.

Librarians seeking to attract and retain the interest of young adolescents look to build collections and develop skills that will help them connect readers to books that will resonate with them. Collection development and reader's advisory for younger teens is most effective when it is grounded in the developmental stages of their young lives. It is in early adolescence that teens begin to make many of their own choices about how they will spend their time, and which of the many competing and attractive areas will capture their imagination. If reading is to be an option, it must satisfy the person the young adolescent is becoming. The physical changes that early adolescents experience are visible to all and remain a primary focus for the adolescents themselves. However, the emotional and psychological changes are just as important as teens seek literature that matters to them. Experts in adolescent literature have long made the connection between adolescent psychology and teen choices in literature. Descriptions of the developmental stages of adolescents remain a centerpiece of any discussion of young adult literature. Current researchers in the field, such as Dr. Thomas Greenspon, outline the important facets of early adolescent development in language accessible to all who work with this age group. Speaking at a recent institute, Dr. Greenspon spoke about these facets as:

1. Social—connections to peers

2. Intellectual—capacity for abstract thinking

3. Focus—ability and motivation to focus on particular activities

4. Adventure/Curiosity—desire for new experiences

5. Sexuality—physical development and capacity for emotional intimacy

6. Self-regulation and definition—capacity to view and present oneself in a certain way.

(Lecture and material given by Thomas Greenspon at ALSC National Institute, Minneapolis, MN; October 1, 2004.)

In addition to the facets of adolescent development, social scientists have been interested in what teens need for a positive coming-of-age experience and in order to develop into healthy adults. Teens need to have positive interactions with their peers and caring adults. They need to have opportunities to learn and master new skills. Young adolescents need to be able to make meaningful contributions to their communities (including schools and families). They need to have places to go that are safe, physically and psychologically.

READING CUES FROM YOUTH DEVELOPMENT

More recently, libraries have begun to apply principles of youth development to their services to teens. The lessons learned from these new approaches have caused libraries to take a critical look at teen spaces, programs and marketing, youth participation, and job and volunteer opportunities for teen customers. Projects such as Public Libraries as Partners in Youth Development (PLPYD), administered by the Urban Libraries Council and funded by the Wallace-Reader's Digest Funds, and publications such as *New Directions for Library Services to Young Adults* by Patrick Jones and the Young Adult Library Services Association of the American Library Association indicate a commitment to bringing library services in line with current research and best practices for working with younger teens. In a PLPYD project, nine libraries developed and implemented programs that actively sought to bring positive youth development principles into their work with young adults. *New Directions for Library Services to Young Adults* emphasizes the importance of understanding adolescent development as a cornerstone of young adult library services.

These ideas also provide guidance for building engaging and relevant collections and reader's advisory services for teens. They give insight into why certain titles and genres resonate with younger teens. How well particular books, along with their characters, themes, and plots, reflect, support, or challenge the development of younger teens provides additional information for those seeking to facilitate positive reading experiences for teens. Indeed, it has been thought that these are many of the reasons that teens read fiction. Current research tells us that all teens share particular needs during their early adolescence. Those seeking to provide useful collections and services to support the reading tastes and interests of these young people will have more success if an understanding of youth development serves as their foundation.

Successful writers for younger teens may not consciously seek to incorporate developmental tasks, as outlined by Dr. Greenspon, or healthy youth development requirements, as articulated by Dr. Konopka, in their writing, but their characters and themes resonate with this audience and reflect these critical areas in teen growth.

Social Development (Family and Peers)

The place of family and friends is a core theme for many books directed at younger teens. Family dynamics that work to promote the healthy development of teens and, more often, those that make that development more difficult, are explored by young adult writers. Finding and interacting with peers and coping with both insider and outsider status is another critical aspect of social development. David Almond's award-winning *Kit's Wilderness* successfully explores issues pertaining to family and friends as Kit seeks to connect with his aging grandfather and relate to a school outsider, John Askew. In *Miracle's Boys* by Jacqueline Woodson, Lafayette relates the attempts made by him and his brothers to remain a family after the death of their parents and the incarceration of their middle brother. The change that occurs when a young man faces the fallibility of a beloved stepfather is gracefully explored in Graham Salisbury's *Lord of the Deep*. Patricia Reilly Giff's *Pictures of Hollis Woods* presents the attempts of a girl to fit into foster families and how difficult it is for young teens to accept themselves in these situations. The challenge of establishing a relationship with a teen outside the peer group is an important aspect of both Jerry Spinelli's *Stargirl* and Koja Kathe's *Buddha Boy*. The issue of bullying and teen response is a major theme of *Indigo's Star* by Hilary McKay even as it portrays a colorful family dynamic.

Books Exploring Social Development

Almond, David. **Kit's Wilderness.** New York: Delacorte, 2000.
Thirteen-year-old Kit goes to live with his grandfather in the decaying coal-mining town of Stoneygate, England, and finds both the old man and the town haunted by ghosts of the past. Winner of the 2001 Michael L. Printz Award.

Bauer, Joan. **Stand Tall.** New York: G.P. Putnam, 2002.
Tree, a six-foot-three-inch twelve-year-old, copes with his parents' recent divorce and his failure as an athlete by helping his grandfather, a Vietnam vet and recent amputee, and Sophie, a new girl at school.

Choldenko, Gennifer. **Al Capone Does My Shirts.** New York: G.P. Putnam, 2004.
A twelve-year-old boy named Moose moves to Alcatraz Island in 1935 when guards' families were housed there, and has to contend with his extraordinary new environment in addition to life with his autistic sister. Newbery Honor Book.

Cohn, Rachel. **The Steps.** New York: Simon & Schuster Books for Young Readers, 2003.
Over Christmas vacation, Annabel goes from her home in Manhattan to visit her father, his new wife, and her half- and step-siblings in Sydney, Australia.

Coman, Carolyn. **Many Stones.** Ashevelle, NC: Front Street, 2000.
After her sister Laura is murdered in South Africa, Berry and her estranged father travel there to participate in the dedication of a memorial in her name. Winner of the 2001 Michael L. Printz Award, and a 2000 National Book Award finalist.

Creech, Sharon. **Granny Torrelli Makes Soup.** New York: Joanna Cotler Books, 2003.

With the help of her wise, old grandmother, twelve-year-old Rosie manages to work out some problems in her relationship with her best friend, Bailey, the boy next door.

Giff, Patricia Reilly. **Pictures of Hollis Woods.** New York: Random House/ Wendy Lamb Books, 2002.

A troublesome twelve-year-old orphan, staying with an elderly artist who needs her, remembers the only other time she was happy in a foster home, with a family that truly seemed to care about her.

Holt, Kimberly Willis. **Keeper of the Night.** New York: Henry Holt, 2003.

Isabel, a thirteen-year-old girl living on the island of Guam, and her family try to cope with the death of Isabel's mother who committed suicide.

Howe, James. **The Misfits.** New York: Atheneum Books for Young Readers, 2001.

Four students who do not fit in at their small-town middle school decide to create a third party for the student council elections to represent all students who have ever been called names.

Hughes, Mark Peter. **I Am the Wallpaper.** New York: Delacorte, 2005.

Thirteen-year-old Floey Packer, jealous of her attractive and popular older sister, shares her home with two younger cousins and experiences a summer vacation filled with embarrassing events, with herself as the star.

Klise, Kate. **Deliver Us from Normal.** New York: Scholastic, 2005.

With a mother who buys Christmas cards in August and a younger brother who describes the Trinity as a toasted marshmallow on a graham cracker, life for eleven-year-old Charles Harrisong is anything but normal in Normal, Illinois.

Koja, Kathe. **Buddha Boy.** New York: Farrar, Straus and Giroux, 2003.

Justin spends time with Jinsen, the unusual and artistic new student whom the school bullies torment and call Buddha Boy, and ends up making choices that impact Jinsen, himself, and the entire school.

Konigsburg, E. L. **Silent to the Bone.** New York: Atheneum Books for Young Readers, 2000.

When he is wrongly accused of gravely injuring his baby half sister, thirteen-year-old Branwell loses his power of speech, and only his friend Connor is able to reach him and uncover the truth about what really happened.

Lynch, Chris. **Gold Dust.** New York: HarperCollins, 2000.

In 1975, twelve-year-old Richard befriends Napolean, a Caribbean newcomer to his Catholic school, hoping that Napolean will learn to love baseball and the Red Sox and will win acceptance in the racially polarized Boston school.

Martin, Ann. **A Corner of the Universe.** New York: Scholastic Press, 2002.
    The summer that Hattie turns twelve, she meets the childlike uncle she never knew and becomes friends with a girl who works at the carnival that comes to Hattie's small town. Newbery Honor Book.

McGhee, Alison. **Snap.** Cambridge, MA: Candlewick Press, 2004.
    Eleven-year-old Edwina confronts old and new challenges when her longtime best friend Sally faces the inevitable death of the grandmother who raised her.

McKay, Hilary. **Indigo's Star.** New York: M.K. McElderry Books, 2003.
    Spurred on by his youngest sister, Rose, twelve-year-old Indigo sticks up for himself and an American boy who has replaced him as the primary target of the school bullies.

Paulsen, Gary. **The Glass Cafe; or, The Stripper and the State: How My Mother Started a War with the System That Made Us Kind of Rich and a Little Bit Famous.** New York: Random House/Wendy Lamb Books, 2003.
    When twelve-year-old Tony, a talented artist, begins sketching the dancers at the Kitty Kat Club where his mother is an exotic dancer, it sparks the attention of social services.

Placide, Jaira. **Fresh Girl.** New York: Random House/Wendy Lamb Books, 2002.
    After having been sent, at a very young age, from New York to live with her grandmother in Haiti, fourteen-year-old Mardi returns to join her parents and tries to shape a new life in Brooklyn.

Salisbury, Graham. **The Lord of the Deep**. New York: Delacorte, 2001.
    Working for his stepfather on a charter fishing boat in Hawaii teaches thirteen-year-old Mikey about fishing, and about taking risks, making sacrifices, and facing some of life's difficult choices.

Spinelli, Jerry. **Stargirl**. New York: Alfred Knopf, 2000.
    In this story about the perils of popularity, the courage of nonconformity, and the thrill of first love, an eccentric student named Stargirl changes Mica High School forever.

White, Ruth. **Memories of Summer**. New York: Farrar, Straus and Giroux, 2000.
    In 1955, thirteen-year-old Lyric finds her whole life changing when her family moves from the hills of Virginia to a town in Michigan and her older sister Summer begins descending into mental illness.

Wolfson, Jill. **What I Call Life.** New York: Henry Holt, 2005.
    Eleven-year-old Cal Lavender learns how to cope with life from the four other girls who live in her group foster home and from their storytelling guardian, the Knitting Lady.

Woodson, Jacqueline. **Miracle's Boys.** New York: G.P. Putnam, 2000.

Twelve-year-old Lafayette's close relationship with his older brother Charlie changes after Charlie is released from a detention home and blames Lafayette for the death of their mother. Winner of the Coretta Scott King Award.

Intellectual Capacity and Decision Making

Learning and the development of decision making in the lives of teens adds a level of understanding about the characters in books they read. As intellectual capacity increases, the complexity of choices in the lives of young teens directly affects the variety and quality of decisions they will need to make. Teen readers are able to observe teen characters coping with difficult challenges and experiencing success and failure in discerning the best decisions for their situations. In *Bucking the Sarge* by Christopher Paul Curtis, winning the school science fair is a prime motivator for Luther T. Farrell. In *True Believer* by Virginia Euwer Wolff, LaVaughn works hard to maintain her place in a program for academically gifted students. Naomi Leon is forced to make important decisions when faced with a mother who seeks to separate her from her younger brother because of his physical deformity, in *Becoming Naomi Leon* by Pam Munoz Ryan. Heidi in Sarah Week's *So B. It* must solve the mystery of her developmentally disabled mother in order to learn where she really belongs.

Books about Intellectual Capacity and Problem Solving

Alexander, Lloyd. **The Gawgon and the Boy**. New York: Dutton's Children's Books, 2001.

In Depression-era Philadelphia, when eleven-year-old David is too ill to attend school, he is tutored by the unique and adventurous Aunt Annie, whose teaching combines with his imagination to greatly enrich his life.

Bloor, Edward. **Story Time**. Orlando: Harcourt, 2004.

George and Kate are promised the best education but instead face obsessed administrators, endless tests, and evil spirits when they are transferred to Whittaker Magnet School.

Boyce, Frank Cottrell. **Millions.** New York: HarperCollins, 2004.

After their mother dies, two brothers find a huge amount of money which they must spend quickly before England switches to the new European currency, but they disagree on what to do with it.

Codell, Esme Raji. **Sahara Special**. New York: Hyperion, 2003.

Struggling with school and her feelings since her father left, Sahara gets a fresh start with a new and unique teacher who supports her writing talents and the individuality of each of her classmates.

Cummings, Priscilla. **Red Kayak**. New York: Dutton, 2004.

Living near the water on Maryland's Eastern Shore, thirteen-year-old Brady and his best friends J.T. and Digger become entangled in a tragedy that tests their friendship and their ideas about right and wrong.

Curtis, Christopher Paul. **Bucking the Sarge.** New York: Wendy Lamb Books, 2004.

Deeply involved in his cold and manipulative mother's shady business dealings in Flint, Michigan, fourteen-year-old Luther keeps a sense of humor while running the Happy Neighbor Group Home for Men, all the while dreaming of going to college and becoming a philosopher.

English, Karen. **Francie**. New York: Farrar, Straus and Giroux, 1999.

When the sixteen-year-old boy whom she tutors in reading is accused of attempting to murder a white man, Francie gets herself in serious trouble for her efforts at friendship. Coretta Scott King Honor winner.

Flake, Sharon. **The Skin I'm In.** New York: Jump at the Sun/Hyperion Books for Children, 1998.

Thirteen-year-old Maleeka, uncomfortable because her skin is extremely dark, meets a new teacher with a birthmark on her face and makes some discoveries about how to love who she is and what she looks like.

Korman, Gordon. **Maxx Comedy: The Funniest Kid in America**. New York: Hyperion Books, 2003.

Eleven-year-old Max Carmody has wanted to be a stand-up comedian since he was five, so when a contest is held to find the "world's funniest kid," he goes through all kinds of craziness to win.

Oppel, Kenneth. **Airborn.** New York: Eos, 2004.

Matt, a young cabin boy with dreams of becoming a pilot, and Kate, a wealthy young girl, team up to search for the existence of mysterious winged creatures reportedly living hundreds of feet above the Earth's surface. Michael Printz Honor book.

Philbrick, W. Rodman. **The Last Book in the Universe**. New York: Scholastic Press/Blue Sky Press, 2000.

After an earthquake has destroyed much of the planet, an epileptic teenager nicknamed Spaz begins the heroic fight to bring human intelligence back to the Earth of a distant future.

Ryan, Pam Munoz. **Becoming Naomi Leone.** New York: Scholastic Press, 2004.

When Naomi's absent mother resurfaces to claim her, Naomi runs away to Mexico with her great-grandmother and younger brother in search of her father. Winner of the Schneider Family Award.

Stauffacher, Sue. **Harry Sue.** New York: Knopf, 2005.

Tough-talking Harry Sue would like to start a life of crime in order to be "sent up" and find her incarcerated mother, but she must first protect the children at her neglectful grandmother's home day care center and befriend a paralyzed boy.

Thomas, Rob. **Green Thumb**. New York: Simon & Schuster Books for Young Readers, 1999.

While spending the summer in the Amazon rain forest of Brazil doing botanical research, thirteen-year-old Grady discovers a secret language used by the trees to communicate with each other and falls afoul of the dictatorial Dr. Carter, whose motives seem questionable.

Weeks, Sarah. **So B. It.** New York: Laura Geringer Books, 2004.

After spending her life with her mentally retarded mother and agoraphobic neighbor, twelve-year-old Heidi sets out from Reno, Nevada, to New York to find out who she is.

Wolff, Virginia Euwer. **True Believer.** New York: Atheneum Books for Young Readers, 2001.

Living in the inner city amidst guns and poverty, fifteen-year-old LaVaughn learns from old and new friends, and inspiring mentors, that life is what you make it—an occasion to rise to. National Book Award winner.

Wynne-Jones, Tim. **The Boy in the Burning House.** New York: Farrar, Straus and Giroux, 2001.

Trying to solve the mystery of his father's disappearance from their rural Canadian community, fourteen-year-old Jim gets help from the disturbed Ruth Rose, who suspects her stepfather, a local pastor.

Focus and Self-Direction

Early adolescence is a period when many teens develop interests that they seek to pursue and which become integral parts of the person they want to become. Characters in books for younger teens often reveal the focus and self-direction that is unfolding in their lives as they move forward. For example, Delia and her friends direct their attention to winning a championship in Sharon Draper's *Double Dutch*. Richard's obsession with baseball is a critical element in *Gold Dust* by Chris Lynch. Jed channels his grief over the death of his older brother by making a documentary about the neighborhood and music that Zeke loved, in *Birdland* by Tracy Mack. In *A Piece of Heaven*, Haley turns her attention to being perfect at her after-school clean-up job as a way to cope with the problems in her family. Ned Begay is able to focus his knowledge of his native Navajo language to become part of the code talkers of World War II in Joseph Bruchac's historical novel, *Code Talker: A Novel about the Navajo Marines of World War II*. Lavinia Fontana defies the role of Renaissance-era women as she seeks to become a painter, in Louise Hawes' *The Vanishing Point: A Story of Lavinia Fontana.*

Books about Focus and Direction

Bauer, Joan. **Backwater.** New York: G.P. Putnam, 1999.

    While compiling a genealogy of her family of successful attorneys, sixteen-year-old history buff Ivy Breedlove treks into the mountain wilderness to interview a reclusive aunt with whom she identifies and who in turn helps her to truly know herself and her family.

Bloor, Edward. **Tangerine.** New York: Scholastic Press, 1997.

    Twelve-year-old Paul, who lives in the shadow of his football hero brother Erik, fights for the right to play soccer despite his near blindness and slowly begins to remember the incident that damaged his eyesight.

Bradley, Kimberly Brubaker. **For Freedom: The Story of a French Spy.** New York: Delacorte, 2003.

    A novel based on the experiences of Suzanne David Hall, who, as a teenager in Nazi-occupied France, worked as a spy for the French resistance while training to be an opera singer.

Creech, Sharon. **Heartbeat.** New York: HarperCollins/Joanna Cotler, 2004.

    Twelve-year-old Annie ponders the many rhythms of life the year that her mother becomes pregnant, her grandfather begins faltering, and her best friend (and running partner) becomes distant.

Flanagan, John. **The Ranger's Apprentice. Book I: The Ruins of Gorlan.** New York: Philomel, 2005.

    When fifteen-year-old Will is rejected by battle school, he becomes the reluctant apprentice to the mysterious Ranger Halt, and winds up protecting the kingdom from danger.

Fleischman, Paul. **Seedfolks.** New York: HarperCollins, 1997.

    One by one, a number of people of varying ages and backgrounds transform a trash-filled inner-city lot into a productive and beautiful garden, and, in doing so, the gardeners are themselves transformed.

Henkes, Kevin. **The Birthday Room.** New York: Greenwillow, 1999.

    When twelve-year-old Ben visits his uncle in Oregon, he feels caught in the strained relationship between his mother and her brother while beginning to accept himself as an artist.

Johnson, Angela. **Bird.** New York: Dial, 2004.

    Devastated by the loss of a second father, thirteen-year-old Bird follows her stepfather from Cleveland to Alabama in hopes of convincing him to come home, and along the way helps two boys cope with their difficulties.

Joseph, Lynn. **The Color of My Words**. New York: HarperCollins/Joanna Cotler Books, 2000.

    When life gets difficult for Ana Rosa, a twelve-year-old would-be writer living in a small village in the Dominican Republic, she can depend on her older brother to make her feel better—until the life-changing events on her thirteenth birthday.

Konigsburg, E. L. **The Outcasts of 19 Schuyler Place.** New York: Atheneum Books for Young Readers, 2004.

    Upon leaving an oppressive summer camp, twelve-year-old Margaret Rose Kane spearheads a campaign to preserve three unique towers her great-uncles have been building in their back yard for more than forty years.

Lubar, David. **Sleeping Freshmen Never Lie.** New York: Dutton, 2005.

    While navigating his first year of high school and awaiting the birth of his new baby brother, Scott loses old friends and gains some unlikely new ones as he hones his skills as a writer.

McNamee, Graham. **Acceleration.** New York: Random House/Wendy Lamb Books, 2003.

    Stuck working in the lost and found department of the Toronto Transit Authority for the summer, seventeen-year-old Duncan finds the diary of a serial killer and sets out to stop him.

Murray, Martine. **The Slightly True Story of Cedar B. Hartley (Who Planned to Live an Unusual Life).** New York: Scholastic Press, 2003.

    When twelve-year-old Cedar loses her dog, it sets off a chain of events leading her to find a new friend, become an acrobat, and learn some bitter-sweet truths about family, community, and herself.

Naidoo, Beverley. **The Other Side of Truth.** New York: HarperCollins, 2001.

    Smuggled out of Nigeria after their mother's murder, Sade and her younger brother are abandoned in London when their uncle fails to meet them at the airport, and they are fearful of their new surroundings and of what may have happened to their journalist father back in Nigeria.

Paterson, Katherine. **The Same Stuff as Stars.** New York: Clarion, 2002.

    When Angel's self-absorbed mother leaves her and her younger brother with their poor great-grandmother, the eleven-year-old girl worries not only about her mother and brother, her imprisoned father, and the frail old woman, but also about a mysterious man who begins sharing with her the wonder of the stars.

Sachar, Louis. **Small Steps.** New York: Delacorte, 2006.

    Three years after being released from Camp Green Lake, Armpit is trying hard to keep his life on track, but when his old pal X-Ray shows up with a tempting plan to make some easy money scalping concert tickets, Armpit reluctantly goes along.

Schmidt, Gary D. **Lizzie Bright and the Buckminster Boy.** New York: Clarion Books, 2004.

In 1911, Turner Buckminster hates his new home of Phippsburg, Maine, but things improve when he meets Lizzie Bright Griffin, a girl from a poor nearby island community founded by former slaves that the town fathers—and Turners—want to change into a tourist spot. Newbery Honor and Printz Honor Awards.

Spinelli, Jerry. **Wringer.** New York: HarperCollins, 1997.

As Palmer comes of age, he must either accept the violence of being a wringer at his town's annual Pigeon Day or find the courage to oppose it. Newbery Honor winner.

Tolan, Stephanie. **Surviving the Applewhites.** New York: HarperCollins, 2002.

Jake, a budding juvenile delinquent, is sent for homeschooling to the arty and eccentric Applewhite family's Creative Academy, where he discovers talents and interests he never knew he had. Newbery Honor winner.

Adventure and Curiosity

Curiosity and an adventuresome spirit are important character traits for the title character of Joan Bauer's *Hope Was Here*. *The Sisterhood of the Traveling Pants* and its sequels by Ann Brashares combine adventure and friendship. Alex Rider, hero of the series that bears his name, beginning with the first book *Stormcatcher*, faces adventure and intrigue. The title character of Richard Mosher's *Zazoo's* curiosity about her grandfather's past leads her to uncover secrets about the residents of her village and facts she did not know about her own heritage. For Skiff, the adventure of capturing a huge fish for money is spurred by his efforts to help his family recover from the loss of his mother, in Rodman Philbrick's *The Young Man and the Sea*. A very different sea adventure is life altering for Sophie in Charon Creech's *The Wanderer*.

Books Exploring Adventure and Curiosity

Creech, Sharon. **Ruby Holler**. New York: HarperCollins/Joanna Cotler Books, 2002.

Thirteen-year-old fraternal twins Dallas and Florida have grown up in a terrible orphanage, but their lives change forever when an eccentric but sweet older couple invites them each on an adventure, beginning in an almost magical place called Ruby Holler.

Curtis, Christopher Paul. **Bud, Not Buddy.** New York: Delacorte, 1999.

Bud, a motherless boy living in Flint, Michigan during the Great Depression, escapes a bad foster home and sets out in search of the man he believes is his father—the renowned bandleader H. E. Calloway of Grand Rapids. Newbery Medal winner.

Giff, Patricia Reilly. **Willow Run.** New York: Wendy Lamb Books, 2005.
> During World War II, after moving with her parents to Willow Run, Michigan, when her father gets a job in the B-24 bomber factory, eleven-year-old Meggie learns about different kinds of bravery from all of the people around her.

Lawrence, Iain. **Ghost Boy.** New York: Delacorte, 2000.
> Unhappy in a home seemingly devoid of love, a fourteen-year-old albino boy who thinks of himself as Harold the Ghost runs away to join the circus, where he works with the elephants and searches for a sense of who he is.

Leavitt, Martine. **Tom Finder.** Calgary, Alta: Red Deer Press, 2003.
> A fifteen-year-old boy living on the streets suddenly cannot remember his past, except for the mysterious significance of Mozart's "The Magic Flute," and when he makes it to a performance of the opera, he is flooded with shocking memories.

Morpurgo, Michael. **Kensuke's Kingdom.** New York: Scholastic Press, 2003.
> When Michael is swept off his family's yacht, he washes up on a desert island, where he struggles to survive—until he finds he is not alone.

Oppel, Kenneth. **Skybreaker.** New York: HarperCollins, 2006.
> Matt Cruse, a student at the Airship Academy, and Kate de Vries, a young heiress, team up with a gypsy and a daring captain to find a long-lost airship, rumored to carry a treasure beyond imagination.

Peterson, P. J. **White Water.** New York: Simon & Schuster Books for Young Readers, 1997.
> Greg confronts his own fears and assumes a leadership role when his father is bitten by a rattlesnake during a white-water rafting trip.

Sexuality and Relationships

Issues concerning sexuality are very important to young adolescents. The physical changes to their bodies are a focal point, as is an understanding of who they are sexually and how they are perceived by other teens. Sexual attraction and an appreciation of themselves and others is the core of developing an overall identity. Exploring these issues through fiction is one way for young adolescents to ask questions and seek answers for a very important topic in their lives. Fictionalized encounters can provide a window into the lives of teens experiencing concerns similar to those of the reader. Sexuality is a very charged topic for many teens to discuss with adults. Fiction can help young adolescents frame questions about the topic.

Establishing a sexual identity is the focus of both Xio and Frederick in Alex Sanchez's *So Hard to Say*. Making sense of a first attraction proves difficult for Martha in *Olive's Ocean* by Kevin Henkes. Becoming a young woman has family and cultural implications for Violet in *Cuba 15* by Nancy Osa. In *Absolutely Normal Chaos* by Sharon Creech, Mary Lou experiences her first romance as she works on her summer journal writing assignment. Fourteen-year-old Staggerlee in *The House You Pass on the Way* by Jacqueline Woodson is coping with being the child of interracial parents. She is also wondering if she might be gay. All of the characters in the ten overlapping stories in Ellen Conford's *Crush* are seeking to establish themselves as attractive as they prepare for the Valentine's Day dance at school.

Books Exploring Sexuality and Relationships

Conford, Ellen. **Crush.** New York: HarperCollins, 1998.
> A series of nine romantic episodes in the lives of B. J. and other students at Cutter's Forge High as they plan for the Valentine's Day Sweetheart Stomp.

Creech, Sharon. **Absolutely Normal Chaos.** New York: HarperCollins, 1995.
> Thirteen-year-old Mary Lou grows up considerably during the summer while learning about romance, homesickness, death, and her cousin's search for his biological father.

Henkes, Kevin. **Olive's Ocean.** New York: Greenwillow, 2003.
> On a summer visit to her grandmother's cottage by the ocean, twelve-year-old Martha gains perspective on the death of a classmate, on her relationship with her grandmother, on her feelings for an older boy, and on her plans to be a writer. Newbery Honor winner.

Osa, Nancy. **Cuba 15.** New York: Delacorte, 2003.
> Violet Paz, a Chicago high school student, reluctantly prepares for her upcoming "quince," a Spanish nickname for the celebration of an Hispanic girl's fifteenth birthday.

Sanchez, Alex. **So Hard to Say.** New York: Simon & Schuster Books for Young Readers, 2004.
> Thirteen-year-old Xio, a Mexican American girl, and Frederick, who has just moved to California from Wisconsin, quickly become close friends, but when Xio starts thinking of Frederick as her boyfriend, he must confront his feelings of confusion and face the fear that he might be gay.

Woodson, Jacqueline. **The House You Pass on the Way.** New York: Delacorte, 1997.
> When fourteen-year-old Staggerlee, the daughter of interracial parents, spends a summer with her cousin Trout, she begins to question her sexuality to Trout and catches a glimpse of her possible future self.

Self-Regulation and Self-Definition

Tessy uses a school assignment to establish a new self-perception, in *The Hero of Ticonderoga* by Gail Gauthier. When Roy connects with the running boy and his sister Beatrice, in Carl Hiaasen's *Hoot*, he finds a cause that allows him to define himself as something other than a bully's victim. Evie's efforts to define herself are complicated by the fact that her family is placed in a witness protection program, in Jacqueline Woodson's *Hush.*

Books Exploring Self-Regulation and Self-Definition

Almond, David. **The Fire-Eaters.** New York: Delacorte, 2004.

> In 1962 England, despite observing his father's illness and the suffering of the fire-eating Mr. McNulty, as well as enduring abuse at school and the stress of the Cuban Missile Crisis, Bobby Burns and his family and friends still find reasons to rejoice in their lives and have hope for the future.

Bauer, Joan. **Rules of the Road.** New York: G.P. Putnam, 1998.

> Sixteen-year-old Jenna gets a job driving the elderly owner of a chain of successful shoe stores from Chicago to Texas to confront the son who is trying to force her to retire. Along the way, Jenna hones her talents as a saleswoman and finds the strength to face her alcoholic father.

Broach, Elise. **Shakespeare's Secret.** New York: Henry Holt, 2005.

> Named after a character in a Shakespeare play, misfit sixth-grader Hero becomes interested in exploring this unusual connection because of a valuable diamond supposedly hidden in her new house, an intriguing neighbor, and the unexpected attention of the most popular boy in school.

Couloumbis, Audrey. **Getting Near to Baby.** New York: G.P. Putnam, 1999.

> Although thirteen-year-old Willa Jo and her aunt Patty seem to be constantly at odds, staying with her and Uncle Hob helps Willa Jo and her younger sister come to terms with the death of their family's baby. Newbery Honor winner.

D'Adamo, Francesco. **Iqbal: A Novel.** Translated by Ann Leonari. New York: Atheneum Books for Young Readers, 2003.

> A fictionalized account of a Pakistani child who escaped from bondage in a carpet factory and went on to help liberate other children like him before being gunned down at the age of thirteen.

Flake, Sharon. **Money Hungry.** New York: Hyperion/Jump at the Sun, 2001.

> All thirteen-year-old Raspberry can think of is making money so that she and her mother never have to worry about living on the streets again. Coretta Scott King Honor.

Hiaasen, Carl. **Hoot.** New York: Alfred Knopf, 2002.

Roy, who is new to his small Florida community, becomes involved in another boy's attempt to save a colony of burrowing owls from a proposed construction site. Newbery Honor winner.

Horvath, Polly. **The Vacation.** New York: Farrar, Straus and Giroux, 2005.

When his parents go to Africa to work as missionaries, twelve-year-old Henry's eccentric aunts, Pigg and Mag, take him on a cross-country car trip, allowing him to gain insight into his family and himself.

Howe, Norma. **The Adventures of Blue Avenger: A Novel.** New York: Henry Holt, 1999.

On his sixteenth birthday, still trying to cope with the unexpected death of his father, David Schumacher decides—or does he—to change his name to Blue Avenger, hoping to find a way to make a difference in his Oakland neighborhood and the world.

Leavitt, Martine. **Heck Superhero.** Asheville, NC: Front Street, 2004.

Abandoned by his mother, thirteen-year-old Heck tries to survive on his own as his mind bounces between the superhero character he imagines himself to be and the harsh reality of his life.

Nelson, Theresa. **Ruby Electric.** New York: Atheneum Books for Young Readers, 2003.

Twelve-year-old Ruby Miller, a movie buff and an aspiring screenwriter, tries to resolve the mysteries surrounding her little brother's stuffed woolly mammoth and their father's five-year absence.

Shusterman, Neal. **The Schwa Was Here.** New York: Dutton, 2004.

A Brooklyn eighth grader nicknamed Antsy befriends the Schwa, an "invisible-ish" boy who is tired of blending into his surroundings and going unnoticed by nearly everyone.

Spinelli, Jerry. **Loser.** New York: HarperCollins/Joanna Cotler Books, 2002.

Even though his classmates from first grade on have considered him strange and a loser, Daniel Zinkoff's optimism and exuberance and the support of his loving family do not allow him to feel that way about himself.

Woodson, Jacqueline. **Hush.** New York: G. P. Putnam, 2002.

Twelve-year-old Toswiah finds her life changed when her family enters the witness protection program. National Book Award finalist.

READING CUES FROM A CHANGING CULTURE

In addition to the personal and societal influences of developmental stages, cultural trends and changes also impact reading tastes and interests of young teens. Popular culture continues to play a large role in what teens seek from libraries. These popular culture influences range from hot topics of interest to younger teens to specific titles that have movie, music, or TV tie-ins. Books with links to movies such as *The Princess Diaries* and *Holes* remain popular with younger adolescents. Libraries with limited budgets are often reluctant to commit resources to this area. However, it is important that teens see some examples of popular culture in the collection. Having these items in the collection lets teens know that their interests are important to the library. This issue may also be an area where young teens can provide critical input and steer library staff to those titles from popular culture that really matter. Dr. Eliza Dresang, in her groundbreaking book *Radical Change: Books for Youth in a Digital Age*, describes how literature for young readers has been forever altered by technology, expansions in formats, and more acceptance of what should be available for young readers. Dr. Dresang refers to three types of "radical change" in books:

Radical Change Type One—Changing Forms and Formats. In this category are books that move away from traditional narratives: novels in verse, documentary novels, novels that employ examples from technology such as e-mail and text messaging. This category also refers to graphic novels and books of fiction that feature illustrations but do not employ strip format.

Radical Change Type Two—Changing Perspectives. This category refers to the culture's receptivity to different voices, novels featuring the voices of teens not previously represented, such as those from different immigrant groups.

Radical Change Type Three—Changing Boundaries. This category refers to books on topics previously seen as taboo or not suitable for younger adolescents. (Dresang, *Radical Change,* p. 17)

Librarians see evidence of these changes in the increased availability of graphic formats; novels that incorporate technological pieces like e-mail and text messaging, such as *The Year of Secret Assignments*; the increased popularity of novels-in-verse such as Printz Honor book *Keesha's House*; and novels based on documents such as *Nothing But the Truth*; even a novel in the form of a screenplay, such as *Monster* by Walter Dean Myers, the winner of the first Printz Award in 2000. Certainly, a novel such as *Bronx Masquerade* by Nikki Grimes, winner of the 2003 Coretta Scott King Award, reflects an acceptance of more inclusion of voices from a variety of ethnic backgrounds. There is certainly more open exploration of all aspects of sexuality. *Luna* by Julie Peters explores a teen coping with her transgendered brother. Alex Sanchez's *So Hard to Say* features middle schoolers coping with issues of sexual identity.

Changing Formats

Avi. **Never Mind.** New York: HarperCollins, 2004.

Twelve-year-old New York City twins Meg and Edward have nothing in common, so they are just as shocked as everyone else when Meg's hopes for popularity and Edward's mischievous schemes coincidentally collide in a hilarious showdown.

Clugston, Chynna. **Queen Bee.** New York: Scholastic Graphix, 2005.
In this graphic novel, a middle school rivalry is complicated by the psychokinetic powers of one of the girls.

Frost, Helen. **Keesha's House.** New York: Farrar, Straus and Giroux, 2003.
Seven teens facing such problems as pregnancy, closeted homosexuality, and abuse each describe in poetic forms what caused them to leave home and where they found home again. Printz Honor winner.

Frost, Helen **Spinning through the Universe: A Novel in Poems from Room 214.** New York: Farrar, Straus and Giroux, 2004.
A collection of poems written in the voices of Mrs. Williams of room 214, her students, and a custodian about their interactions with each other, their families, and the world around them. Includes notes on the poetic forms represented.

Grimes, Nikki. **Bronx Masquerade.** New York: Dial Books, 2002.
While studying the Harlem Renaissance, students at a Bronx high school read aloud poems they have written, revealing their innermost thoughts and fears to their formerly clueless classmates. Coretta Scott King Award winner.

Grimes, Nikki. **What about Good-bye.** New York: Hyperion, 2004.
Alternating poems by a brother and sister convey their feelings about the death of their older brother and the impact it had on their family.

Lester, Julius. **Day of Tears: A Novel in Dialogue.** New York: Hyperion/Jump at the Sun, 2005.
Emma has taken care of the Butler children since Sarah and Frances's mother, Fanny, left. Emma wants to raise the girls to have good hearts, as a rift over slavery has ripped the Butler household apart. Now, to pay off debts, Pierce Butler wants to cash in his slave "assets," possibly including Emma. Coretta Scott King Award winner.

Myers, Walter Dean. **Monster.** New York: HarperCollins, 1999.
While on trial as an accomplice to a murder, sixteen-year-old Steve Harmon records his experiences in prison and in the courtroom in the form of a film script as he tries to come to terms with the course his life has taken. Winner of Printz Award and Coretta Scott King Honor.

Perkins, Lynn Rae. **Criss Cross.** New York: Greenwillow, 2005.
Teenagers in a small town in the 1960s experience new thoughts and feelings, question their identities, connect and disconnect as they search for the meaning of life and love. Newbery winner.

Woodson, Jacqueline. **Locomotion.** New York: Penguin Putnam/G.P. Putnam, 2003.

Inspired by his teacher, eleven-year-old Lonnie begins to write about his life in a series of poems in which he discusses his feelings about his friends, his foster mom, his little sister Lili, and the death of his parents. National Book Award finalist.

Changing Perspectives

Adoff, Jamie. **Jimi and Me.** New York: Hyperion/Jump at the Sun, 2005.

Keith, thirteen and biracial, is plunged into a new existence following the murder of his father and a move to a small town. Coretta Scott King/John Steptoe Award.

Auseon, Andrew. **Funny Little Monkey.** Orlando: Harcourt, 2005.

Arty, an abnormally short fourteen-year-old boy, enlists the help of a group of students, known at school as the "pathetic losers," to take revenge against his abusive, tall fraternal twin brother.

Canales, Viola. **The Tequila Worm.** New York: Random House, 2005.

Sofia grows up in the close-knit community of the barrio in McAllen, Texas, until she finds that her experiences as a scholarship student at an Episcopal boarding school in Austin only strengthen her ties to family and her "comadres." Pura Belpre Award winner.

Curry, Jane Louise. **The Black Canary.** NewYork: McElderry, 2005.

As the child of two musicians, twelve-year-old James has no interest in music until he discovers a portal to seventeenth-century London in his uncle's basement. He finds himself in a situation where his beautiful voice and the fact that he is biracial might serve him well.

Erdrich, Louise. **The Game of Silence.** New York: HarperCollins, 2005.

Nine-year-old Omakayas, of the Ojibwa tribe, moves west with her family in 1849 after her village is threatened by white leaders.

Flake, Sharon. **Bang!** New York: Hyperion/Jump at the Sun, 2005.

A teenage boy must face the harsh realities of inner city life, a disintegrating family, and destructive temptations as he struggles to find his identity as a young man.

Gallego Garcia, Laura. **The Legend of the Wandering King.** New York: Scholastic/Arthur A. Levine, 2005.

Motivated by jealousy and the desire to receive acclaim as a great poet, Walid ibn Huyr, a prince of ancient Arabia, commits acts that completely change the course of his life.

Grimes, Nikki. **Dark Sons.** New York: Hyperion/Jump at the Sun, 2005.

Alternating poems compare and contrast the conflicted feelings of Ishmael, son of the Biblical patriarch Abraham, and Sam, a teenager in New York City, as they try to come to terms with being abandoned by their fathers and the love they feel for their younger stepbrothers. Coretta Scott King Honor.

Salisbury, Graham. **Eyes of the Emperor.** New York: Wendy Lamb Books, 2005.

Several young Japanese American servicemen during World War II learn that their special assignment is to train K-9 units to hunt Asians.

Yee, Lisa. **Stanford Wong Flunks Big Time.** New York: Scholastic/Arthur A. Levine, 2005.

After flunking sixth-grade English, basketball prodigy Stanford Wong must struggle to pass his summer-school class, keep his failure a secret from his friends, and satisfy his academically demanding father.

Changing Boundaries

Amateau, Gigi. **Claiming Georgia Tate.** Cambridge, MA: Candlewick, 2005.

Twelve-year-old Georgia Tate feels loved and safe living with Nana and Granddaddy, until her sexually abusive father tries to win custody of her.

Crutcher, Chris. **The Sledding Hill.** New York: Greenwillow Books, 2005.

Billy, recently deceased, keeps an eye on his best friend, fourteen-year-old Eddie, who has added to his home and school problems by becoming mute, and helps him stand up to a conservative minister and English teacher who is orchestrating a censorship challenge.

Fensham, Elizabeth. **Helicopter Man.** New York: Bloomsbury, 2005.

Pete finds he must often assume the parenting role when his father's paranoia gets out of control.

Fuqua, Jonathan Scott. **King of the Pygmies.** Cambridge, MA: Candlewick, 2005.

After hearing what he believes are other people's thoughts, high school sophomore Penn learns that he may have schizophrenia and makes some important decisions about how to live his life.

Griffin, Adele. **Where I Want to Be.** New York: G.P. Putnam, 2005.

Two teenaged sisters, separated by death but still connected, work through their feelings of loss over the closeness they shared as children that was later destroyed by one's mental illness, and finally make peace with each other. National Book Award finalist.

Hautman, Pete. **Godless.** New York: Simon & Schuster, 2004.

When sixteen-year-old Jason Bock and his friends create their own religion to worship the town's water tower, what started out as a joke begins to take on a power of its own. National Book Award winner.

Hautman, Pete. **Invisible.** New York: Simon & Schuster, 2005.

Doug and Andy are unlikely best friends—one a loner obsessed by his model trains, the other a popular student involved in football and theater—who grew up together and share a bond that nothing can sever.

Horvath, Polly. **The Caning Season.** New York: Farrar, Straus and Giroux, 2003.

Thirteen-year-old Ratchet spends a summer in Maine with her eccentric great-aunts Tilly and Penpen, hearing strange stories from the past and encountering a variety of unusual and colorful characters.

Howe, James. **Totally Joe.** New York: Atheneum, 2005.

As a school assignment, a thirteen-year-old boy writes an alpha-biography—life from A to Z—and explores issues of friendship, family, school, and the challenges of being a gay teenager.

Larochelle, David. **Absolutely Positively Not.** New York: Scholastic/Arthur A. Levine, 2005.

Steven makes many humorous attempts to fit in at his Minnesota high school by becoming a macho, girl-loving, playboy pinup-displaying heterosexual.

Peters, Julie Ann. **Luna.** New York: Little, Brown, 2004.

Fifteen-year-old Regan's life, which has always revolved around keeping her older brother Liam's transsexuality a secret, changes when Liam decides to start the process of "transitioning" by first telling his family and friends that he is a girl who was born in a boy's body. National Book Award finalist.

Volponi, Paul. **Black and White.** New York: Viking, 2005.

Two star high school basketball players, one black and the other white, experience the justice system differently after committing a crime together and getting caught.

Whyman, Matt. **Boy Kills Man.** New York: HarperCollins/Harper Tempest, 2005.

Thirteen-year-old Sonny has to grow up quickly to cope with the violent streets of Medellin, Colombia.

Woodson, Jacqueline. **Behind You.** New York: G.P. Putnam, 2004.

After fifteen-year-old Jeremiah is mistakenly shot by police, the people who love him struggle to cope with their loss as they recall his life and death, unaware that 'Miah is watching over them.

Zevin, Gabrielle. **Elsewhere.** New York: Farrar, Straus and Giroux, 2005.

> After fifteen-year-old Liz Hall is hit by a taxi and killed, she finds herself in a place that is both like and unlike Earth, where she must adjust to her new status and figure out how to "live."

CONCLUSION

Librarians seeking to build collections and provide reader's advisory for young adolescents will have more success when they center their efforts in the two areas of most critical importance to their customers: youth development and influences from popular culture. The books that resonate with teen readers are those that connect with them on a developmental level and those that reflect their affinity with the culture around them. Librarians who are able to provide and promote these kind of collections will find young readers eager to engage in book discussions, review committees, and teen advisory committees that make the reading experience more than a passive activity.

WORK CITED

Dresang, Eliza. *Radical Change: Books for Youth in a Digital Age.* New York: H. W. Wilson, 1999.

and leisure reading or listening materials, but also by caring enough to
xtras. Most libraries have a core group of youth who hang out there,
. Parents are not back from work until 6 p.m., they do not have a home
ter or quiet place to study, or they may even genuinely like the library
ment. Special programs give these youth something to do, a little in-
al exploration and fun, as well as a chance to become involved. In the
Libraries Council's evaluation consultation of teen perceptions of the
library, it was revealed that libraries could help reverse their stodgy image
by allowing teens to help with activities (Meyers 1999).

Think back to when you were a young adolescent. Where did you spend
time after school? Hangout choices for young adolescents are limited.
are not driving, and many are not yet allowed to wander far from school
ome. The library is perceived as a safe place by caregivers. Young ado-
ts want to participate in events, along with friends. Many, especially those
to junior high, welcome the prospect of meeting new companions who
similar interests. They want to learn fresh skills and be stimulated, but out
school context. The library is neutral territory in which young patrons are
ed and encouraged to explore choice topics free from the pressures of
s, tests, and authority figures. This stimulation comes not just from books
Web sites but also from programs that subtly or explicitly teach, inform, or
tain young adolescents side by side with peers.

An often-cited statistic is that young adults comprise 23 percent of library
nage (Jones, Gorman, and Suellentrop 2004). Youth programming in-
ses the library's visibility by allowing an opportunity to promote collec-
s, partner with the community, and support youth involvement. And, it can
ire youth to tell their friends about the unexpectedly cool stuff going on!

RIEF HISTORY OF TEEN PROGRAMMING

Library services to young adults gained national attention as early as 1929
en the American Library Association (ALA) founded a division of the Chil-
n's Library Association called the Young People's Reading Roundtable. In
49, this merged into the Association for Young People's Librarians. During
s time, ALA published a set of guidelines for YA services, entitled *The Public*
rary Plans for the Teen Age. Emphasis shifted from not only meeting the
ding needs of teens but also exploring how libraries could support their
creational and curricular interests. In 1957 the Young Adult Services Division
ASD), now the Young Adult Library Services Association (YALSA), was
unded. This independence of the young adult library division within the
merican Library Association solidified the value of teen patrons.

Along with many other cultural shifts, the 1960s brought new dimensions t
brary programming. Facilities were built to accommodate multimedia present
ons. Buildings were creatively decorated and made less stodgy. Urban librar
perated satellite sites for young adults, decorated with modish posters of the

4

Programming for 'Tweens and Young Teens

Robyn Lupa

With growing concern about how young people spend their out-of-school time, libraries should not be underestimated in their ability to offer constructive opportunities for teenagers and provide valuable services to the community.—(http://www.wallacefunds.org/WF/News Room/NewsRoom/PressRelease/YouthLibraryProgramsHelp.htm)

Why make the time, expend the effort, and delegate resources to plan programs for young adolescents? Children who enjoyed years of story times, summer reading clubs, and entertaining activities in the children's department should not have to cease the fun simply because they graduate from fifth grade. Elementary school kids hang out at the library because it is perceived as an enjoyable and welcoming place. Once kids hit junior high, the library is not cool anymore (unless we provide ample computers for the whole gang to log on to *Runescape*, or the latest hot multiplayer online role playing game, at 3:15 p.m.). Early adolescence is a crucial time to remind teens that the library acknowledges their growth by providing customized enrichment opportunities. We must strive to create positive interactions for young adolescents so that they will want to continue to use the library. A worthy goal is to inspire young adolescents to view us as a community center, not only by providing computers, homework materials, and in-demand leisure reading or listening materials, but also by caring enough to offer extras. Most libraries have a core group of youth who hang out there, anyway. Parents are not back from work until 6 p.m., they do not have a home computer or quiet place to study, or they may even genuinely like the library environment. Special programs give these youth something to do, a little intellectual exploration and fun, as well as a chance to become involved. In the Urban Libraries Council's evaluation consultation of teen perceptions of the public library, it was revealed that libraries could help reverse their stodgy image simply by allowing teens to help with activities (Meyers 1999).

Think back to when you were a young adolescent. Where did you spend your time after school? Hangout choices for young adolescents are limited. They are not driving, and many are not yet allowed to wander far from school and home. The library is perceived as a safe place by caregivers. Young adolescents want to participate in events, along with friends. Many, especially those new to junior high, welcome the prospect of meeting new companions who share similar interests. They want to learn fresh skills and be stimulated, but out of the school context. The library is neutral territory in which young patrons are allowed and encouraged to explore choice topics free from the pressures of grades, tests, and authority figures. This stimulation comes not just from books and Web sites but also from programs that subtly or explicitly teach, inform, or entertain young adolescents side by side with peers.

An often-cited statistic is that young adults comprise 23 percent of library patronage (Jones, Gorman, and Suellentrop 2004). Youth programming increases the library's visibility by allowing an opportunity to promote collections, partner with the community, and support youth involvement. And, it can inspire youth to tell their friends about the unexpectedly cool stuff going on!

BRIEF HISTORY OF TEEN PROGRAMMING

Library services to young adults gained national attention as early as 1929 when the American Library Association (ALA) founded a division of the Children's Library Association called the Young People's Reading Roundtable. In 1949, this merged into the Association for Young People's Librarians. During this time, ALA published a set of guidelines for YA services, entitled *The Public Library Plans for the Teen Age*. Emphasis shifted from not only meeting the reading needs of teens but also exploring how libraries could support their recreational and curricular interests. In 1957 the Young Adult Services Division (YASD), now the Young Adult Library Services Association (YALSA), was founded. This independence of the young adult library division within the American Library Association solidified the value of teen patrons.

Along with many other cultural shifts, the 1960s brought new dimensions to library programming. Facilities were built to accommodate multimedia presentations. Buildings were creatively decorated and made less stodgy. Urban libraries operated satellite sites for young adults, decorated with modish posters of the day and equipped with record players, paperbacks, and thrift store furniture. These community centers, many operated by advisory groups, took off around the country. More than just hangouts, they served as host sites for discussions on volatile topics of the day. One program planner in California invited hippies to respond to questions on their lifestyle and feelings about the Vietnam War.

Fresh from the 1960s revolution, JoAnn V. Rogers wrote in her 1973 publication *Libraries and Young Adults,* "[P]rogramming for entertainment now is generally accepted in the YA area. . . . Popular culture has become more significant in the shaping of recreational program content. YA specialists are expected to be in tune with what is happening with teenagers in order to . . . provide popular programming." The credibility of young adult library services increased on a national level when the YASD sent delegates to the 1960 and 1971 White House Conference on youth. In conjunction with an ALA preconference on audiovisual materials for young adults, a pamphlet entitled "Mixed Means Programming for Young Adults" was published by YASD. The 1980s saw the production of resource guides for librarians, such as *Youth Participation in School and Public Libraries Manual* and *Youth Participation in Libraries: A Training Manual.* A 1987 preconference, "Courtly Love in the Shopping Mall: Library Programming for Young Adults with a Humanities Focus," resulted from a National Endowment for the Humanities grant that allowed for regional training workshops on this topic.

Mary K. Chelton, currently a professor at the Graduate School of Library and Information Studies, Queens College, New York, offered a wise definition of teen programming in 1975. She stated, "A library sponsored or cosponsored event, inside or outside the library itself, usually well planned but sometimes spontaneous, which appeals for a variety of reasons to a group . . . informational and/or recreational in nature and can be combined with or totally divorced from . . . traditional library activities" (Chelton 1975).

YALSA's 1993 publication entitled *Directions for Library Services to Young Adults* set a philosophical direction for services to teens. It contrasts teens, who find themselves in control of their own time, with children, who are scheduled by parents. Unlike the guaranteed young audiences that appear for children's puppet shows or musical performances, libraries have to assess and respond to a wide variety of teen interests in order to ensure attendance. Today, programming has become an accepted part of regular service to teens in the public library, supported by YALSA on a detailed section of its Professional Development Center Web site http://www.ala.org/ala/yalsa/profdev/programm ingyoung.htm.

UNDERSTANDING YOUNG ADOLESCENTS

Young adolescents are busy composing personal declarations of independence. Some milestones they experience between the ages of ten and fourteen include the following:

- A peer group that suddenly dominates their time and interests. Friends, and the security of belonging to a group, are more important than ever. The herd provides normalcy and validity.

- At the same time, the expression of autonomy and individuality is crucial. Suddenly, young adolescents feel empowered to experiment with everything that was previously comfortable, including speech, companions, dress, music, hobbies, spirituality, and beliefs.

- Because of their attention to and from friends, young adolescents seek independence from family. The peer group gives acceptance and support that is not always obtained at home.

- This goes hand-in-hand with defiant or rebellious behavior as new interests are explored. Hormonal changes cause moodiness. Attitudes vary from week to week with the introduction of so many new individuals, cliques, and social politics.

- Ego dominates a young adolescent's worldview. Issues are frequently seen in black and white.

- Boys and girls experience an enhanced concern about their appearance. Through trial and error, they explore different personas and identities. Many are self-conscious and have a wavering self-esteem.

Visit the *Search Institute's* Web site at www.search-institute.org to read much more about the developmental aspects of teens. Connections between these generalizations and how libraries can employ them in program planning become clear:

- Librarians can support young adults by acting as positive role models.

- Youth are empowered when they help with program preparation.

- The library can coach youth on social expectations by asking them to exhibit appropriate behavior during events.

- Libraries can offer youth a constructive use of time by providing safe settings for organized activities.

- Youth need to make a commitment to learning. The library offers an environment both fun and stimulating with multipurpose collections.

- Through their contributions, youth volunteers internalize positive values and social competencies. The ideas and the skills they bring to programming are appreciated and incorporated.

Young adolescents are seeking creative outlets, self-expression, physical activity, and meaningful activities, all of which may be explored by programming.

PROGRAMMING FOR TEENS

Initial Planning

Now that you have had a quick overview of the psychology of those in the stage of early adolescence, let us explore some ways to generate both fun and practical program ideas. To start, take a bare bones look at the makeup of your community. What are people in this age range doing when not at the library? Where are they shopping? Will you need to lure girls away from hanging at the mall? Maybe a workshop on homemade beauty products will attract them. Is Starbucks flooded with young adolescents after school? If so, why? Is it just the lattes, or do the communal atmosphere, background music, and ample space to congregate have appeal? You may discover captive audiences by duplicating a coffeehouse in the library. What extracurricular activities do youth engage in? Are there lots of college-bound people, or is the majority of the community looking forward to vocational school? A job-hunting clinic is useful for everyone. What is the culture of local schools? Does the entire town attend high school football games? Bring in a homegrown college pro to talk about his career path. Perhaps the competition-winning chess club or quiz bowl teams enjoy the spotlight more than sports. Inspire their competitive spirit by hosting trivia contests and game nights. What are the very specific interests and activities of your area? Perhaps they are rodeos, stock cars, snowboarding, surfing, or mountaineering? Tie programs into those events or activities. Are civics classes talking up the current election? Host a panel political discussion and mock vote. Program possibilities abound.

One of the best aspects of young adult librarianship is that we can consider watching MTV and reading *Teen Vogue* to be job related! Do the magazines forecast that braids are going to be the hit style this summer? Call your local salon and arrange for a hands-on demo. *Dance Dance Revolution* shows no signs of fading? Borrow an X-Box from a regular patron and sponsor a contest. Oscars coming up? Buy a case of popcorn, advertise a movie afternoon, and view the PG-13 rated contenders. Keep up with trends by regularly scanning the following sites: http://www.nexgenlibrarian.net/popculture, www.teenpeople .com, and www.cyberteens.com.

Use valuable professional resources to generate ideas. Read each issue of *VOYA*, especially their annual *Teen Program Roundup* in October. Other library journals, such as *Young Adult Library Services* and *School Library Journal,* also provide ideas for programming.

Check the return carts to determine what is circulating. Learn about young adolescents in your service area by scrutinizing their borrowing habits. What subjects are they pursuing? Witchcraft, astrology, true crime, vegetarianism, skateboarding, beauty, drawing, and NASCAR may be a few. If the waiting lists for top forty CDs are sky high, you will probably attract ample interest in a karaoke night. Do you have a group of young adolescents with more alternative tastes? A concert from an up-and-coming indie band is a sure-fire hit. Knitting is cool right now. Think about what other hobbies are hot. Youth are not easily burned out on popular fads, so capitalize on the anime craze as much as possible by offering drawing, cell painting, and lectures from local comic experts. Patrick Jones suggests that librarians plan programs based on the Dewey Decimal System (Jones, Gorman, and Suellentrop 2004), so browse your nonfiction shelves and notice what topics stand out. Can you plan a program around them?

Promotion

Program marketing is essential for any audience, but mostly when trying to attain young adolescents. Flyers and posters help, especially if you can get them out to schools or even directly into their print and electronic newsletters. Use blogs and look at www.blogwithoutalibrary.net to find out how libraries are using them. Then create a free one at www.blogspot.com, www.Bravenet.com, www.Bravejournal.com, or www.Livejournal.com. Advertise on a blog and encourage young adolescents to post comments on programs or contribute ideas. Check out www.sellerslibraryteens.blogspot.com, http://pplya.blogspot.com/ and http://www.apl.lib.in.us/yablog.html for successful blogging examples. E-mail your library media specialists and teacher contacts, asking them to help with endorsements, especially if they can award extra credit for attendance. Are you hosting an anime workshop? Bring posters to art teachers and ask them to give bonus points to kids who bring in a finished product. Make an attendance list of participants at your evening poetry cafe and e-mail it to teachers the next morning. Post flyers in out-of-the-ordinary places such as comic books stores and CD shops. Does McDonald's or Starbucks have a neighborhood bulletin board? Definitely post library information there. Depending on your community, deposit them in any possible hangout, including coffee shops, recreation centers, and any other nearby places. If you have an in-house graphics department, ask them to create a splashy advertisement and place it in community newspapers. If not, recruit an artistic youth to make a poster and use the color copier at Kinkos. Request a listing on your cable access channel. Parents might watch it. If you have got the resources, send program information to the major newspapers, radio and TV stations. You just may have a surprise visit from the local news, which is a fantastic advertisement for the library.

Despite all of this, the most effective marketing method is word of mouth. While handing a young adolescent a flyer, talk up the program. Tell him how cool it will be to see a uniformed SWAT team, and encourage him to bring friends. Inform the girls who congregate at CD listening stations every afternoon that you are going to hire a guy to airbrush T-shirts, but there are limited numbers of participant slots! There is no doubt that you will find yourself planning programs with names and faces already in mind. Be sure to get their buy-in immediately and urge them to bring the whole gang.

Outreach

When possible, leave the building. Outreach serves a dual purpose: it allows you to promote the library's collections and services, as well as to directly bring library resources into the community. Most of us visit schools regularly to give booktalks, read aloud, or talk up the summer reading club. These are passive acts for the audience, during which library staff are talking at or presenting to them. But active programming such as book discussion groups may be held where teens congregate. Find out what clubs meet after school, and offer to facilitate monthly theme-based book groups on their own turf. Schedule yourself for biweekly outreach to summer day camps. Read a couple of eternally popular Jon Scieszka stories or a teasing chapter from the latest YA best seller. Booktalk some other hot titles and distribute a list of them. Bring along some drawing and origami books, paper, and colored pencils. Ask participants to design something to share with one another and take home. For those who are not feeling creative, pack cool magazines for browsing. Not only are participants engaged in an activity, but you are also making a personal connection and introducing them to a library that offers much more than homework help. This is a perfect opportunity to bring your current newsletter and plug events back at the branch. As Patrick Jones writes, "Given the difficulty of arranging teens' schedules along with access issues, it just makes more sense for one librarian to travel, then expecting ten, twenty, or two hundred teens to do so" (Jones, Gorman, and Suellentrop 2004).

If your library is fortunate enough to fund a big-name author or performer, host that A-level program in a large place such as a school or community auditorium. Some libraries organize summer reading club parties outside of the library. Depending on the number of participants, venues could range from a Pizza Hut to a space in the mall to renting out the whole zoo.

Use the Children's Department as a Resource

Teen and children's programming share a common goal: they are planned according to a target audience and provide a diversion from the patron's normal library routine. Your coworkers in the children's department will most likely have programming down to a science. While they probably try to spread the wealth by hiring different performers each year, their basic topics are pretty consistent: music, puppets, creative movement or drama, art, magic, science. Nevertheless, bounce ideas off of them. After all, it is their former patrons that you are now trying to capture. Observe juvenile programs and talk to the fifth and sixth graders who are accompanying siblings. Ask them what sort of events—without the little kids—would be alluring. Take a look at the notebooks or file folders of ideas that the children's staff has maintained. They probably receive tons of mail from potential presenters. Much of this talent is happy to modify programs for specific age ranges. The favorite drawing guy hired year after year should not be limited to showing second graders how to make simple cartoons. He can easily adapt to instruct teens on drawing elaborate mythological creatures. Is a puppeteer doing a show this summer? Ask him to also host a workshop for young adolescents on creating and maneuvering puppets and building simple stages. Then have your participants put on their own performance in the children's room. Invite a group of young adolescents to learn advanced techniques from your favorite face painter or balloon maker so that they may help during the end-of-summer celebration party.

Despite the crossover appeal of programs such as juggling and magic, young adolescents will not want children in their events. Segregate programs to preserve sacred spaces for teens and those in the stage of early adolescence.

Collaborating with Other Agencies

Schedule yourself to visit a PTA meeting or a church youth group and get them excited about the summer reading club and all of its accompanying fun activities. Remind the audience that the program is free! You can dig up great ideas by looking around the neighborhood. Here are some examples.

- Ask a member of the sheriff's department to bring in a bloodhound and describe the dog's job duties. Find a police officer qualified to talk about Internet safety (and then screen *Hackers*).

- A large component of children's librarianship is the welcoming of elementary school kids into the library for orientations. Why stop at fifth or sixth grade? Invite classes of young people just entering junior high, along with parents, for an introduction to the teen and reference resources at your library. Give a tour, serve snacks, and offer a general Q&A session with several staff members so that they can become familiar faces to the kids. Inviting a multitude of social services agencies to talk about common early adolescent issues during a tough transition period may even expand this program.

- Museums often offer very professional and age-appropriate canned events that are refreshingly low-maintenance for the programmer. Popular topics may include ancient Egypt, astronomy, or visiting artists who come armed with briefcases full of supplies to make, for example, mobiles inspired by Alexander Calder.

- Ask members of the symphony or opera to offer a smaller-scale production in your meeting room or out on the lawn.

- If you can score it, teens will flock to a visit from a highly visible athlete.

- Ask a local martial arts studio to talk about the history of their sport, do some flashy demonstrations and allow the participants to learn some moves. Permit them to set up a table with business cards, Web site address, and flyers. They may recruit prospective students following the program.

- Get to know staff at local hobby shops. Introduce youth to the world of scrap booking and let them come away with a few finished pages.

- Similarly, partner with beauty shops. Not only can they give young adolescent girls a boost of self-esteem, they will also probably gain new clients.

- Ask restaurants to donate coupons for prizes and snacks. Hit up other local merchants for contributions. Offering door prizes, awards, and summer reading club incentives are a sure-fire way to attract attention.

SAMPLE PROGRAMS

Keeping in mind the developmental stages of adolescence, as well as a general public library mission to support the informational and recreational interests of young adolescents, lots of program ideas may be generated. Here are some broad categories.

Practical and Educational

- Host a summer jobs workshop, marketed specifically for the 12- to 15-year-old crowd. Have someone from the local job corps review current or upcoming employment opportunities as well as domestic employment referrals (yard work, housekeeping, babysitting). Then break out into sessions that will teach kids about reading want ads, filling out applications, resume writing, recruiting references, interviewing skills, and the all-important how to dress and behave during an interview as well as on the job. Hook up a computer and projection screen to look at online resources for future career planning, such as www.myfuture.com. Do not forget to announce paid and volunteer opportunities within the library system.

- During winter science fair months, invite a "Mad Science" type group to perform wacky experiments, then ask seasoned teachers or high school mentors to participate in a Q&A on project resources. Ask them to demonstrate simple and practical experiments as well. Pull out all of your materials and database fact sheets for display. Invite parents to this one so that together they can be informed on how to complete a successful science project.

- Young adolescents are itching to babysit and will be even more marketable if officially trained or at least exposed to proper techniques from those who are certified. Negotiate an affordable fee so that the American Red Cross, YMCA, or a local hospital can present a workshop at your facility. Another option is to have various agencies come in to present different pieces. For instance, police and fire departments and a nurse could talk about topics relevant to babysitting. Ask the social services agency to recommend a daycare provider who is qualified to talk about the important developmental stages of young children as well as simple activities to do with them. Cover other basics such as appropriate snacks and even how to change a diaper.

- Is it election season? Ask young adolescents to vote a literary character into the Oval Office. Offer them specific names on a ballot and, in addition to marking one with an X, list three reasons why that character exemplifies leadership qualities. Naturally, have books on display. Choose a few ballots from a hat and award the winners paperbacks to keep. Advertise with mock election posters and even cheap buttons. This would be an ideal partnership with local schools. In between voting, sneak in a panel discussion on the upcoming election. Check out http://www.teenpowerpolitics.com/ for ideas.

- Tie programming directly into the curriculum. Ask teachers to give you a heads up on upcoming projects. Then, plan a program on those topics: mythology, Native Americans, how to deliver a monologue, or plan a cultural festival.

- Hire a Mary Kay or Avon cosmetics consultant to give basic hair care and skin care tips to teens. Ask for volunteers willing to receive a quick makeover. Give away samples that girls can take to share with their mom.

- Explore wellness topics with entertainment thrown in. Ask someone from a health food store to talk about positive eating habits, along with lots of delicious samples. Give cooking tips—how can cookies be baked with added nutrition? Which juice brands are preferable? Are some chocolate bars actually healthy? Maybe some participants will be willing to try tofu for the first time! Combine this with a showcase of various exercises. Have a staff member from the recreation center show the teens basic pilates and yoga moves, point out good running trails in the area, and compare the benefits of various exercise programs.

- Ask high school honor students or a local fraternity to offer homework help after school. Create a flyer advertising days and times during which young adolescents may drop in to ask questions on any topic. While the tutors earn volunteer credits, your teens are getting much-needed help for free.

- Bring in a speaker. Does one of the *Survivor* cast members live in your area? Enlist her to talk about all of the wild experiences on the show. How about local Olympics participants or politicians?

Moving and Doing

- Establish a summer arts workshop, during which participants may write, draw, construct, and—most of all—share their progress. At the end, turn the teen space into an art gallery and host an open mike evening. Recruit guest speakers from the community—guitarists, visual artists, poets—to discuss their creative path.

- Put your squeamishness aside and plan a Fear Factor program for brave competitors and an audience complete with egg tosses, trust falls, and races to eat foods that may be safe but *look* utterly disgusting. Be creative with jello. Buy some of the least appealing flavors of baby food. Go to ethnic markets to purchase foods that many kids will not recognize. An anchovy out of context could be really gross! Use *Gross Grub: Retch-Ed Recipes That Taste Heavenly but Look Like Heck* (Porter 1995) for some amusing inspiration. Open or close the program with a reading of significant passages from *How to Eat Fried Worms*. (Be sure to have parents fill out permission slips for any program involving food. Also, beware of peanut butter or any other food that may cause allergic reactions.)

- There are so many craft program ideas. Find people at hobby stores or even among the library staff who have hidden talents and skills to share. Encourage groups of friends to sign up together for a creative activity. Ideas include making jewelry out of hemp, beading, greeting card design, rubber stamping, scrap booking, tie-dyeing, mehndi, airbrushing t-shirts, making aromatherapy products, journaling, and knitting. Define the number of participants in advance and either give tickets or put names on a list so that you can adequately purchase or acquire supplies. For any ink-on-skin programs, tell teens that they must bring a signed permission slip from parents.

- A fun seasonal program is *Embellish the Holidays*, in which participants are guided to make glittery greeting cards, ornaments, and stamped wrapping paper. Watch out—adults will be clamoring for a similar program of their own!

- Knitting clubs do not have to be adult-only. Start one for teens and open your meeting room to them regularly. Provide snacks to share and play soft music. With permission from the teens, it might be ok to invite moms to this one. Check out the book *Teen Knitting Club: Chill Out and Knit* (Wenger 2004) for lots of ideas.

- Host an always-popular and amusing Duct Tape craft program. Who knew that objects such as shoes, wallets, flowers, and hats can be constructed from Duct Tape? Use Web sites like http://yapp.us/DuctTape .html and www.ducttapeguys.com as well as books such as *Got Tape* (Schiedermayer 2002) and *Ductigami* (Wilson 1999) to plan your event.

- Anything related to food will generate a crowd, such as ethnic cooking (taps into that annual assignment in which kids have to choose an ethnic recipe and write a report on that culture), chocolate molds or smoothie making. During the holidays, ask a representative from the local cooking school to teach teens how to make gingerbread houses. Order in large cheese pizzas from local establishments, and have participants take a blind taste test and mark their choices on ballots.

- Mystery Theater! The drama kids will love this one. If you have a small budget, purchase a do-it-yourself kit from http://acemurdermystery.com or a library vendor. Turn it into a dinner theater by serving pizza and soda. To make things more dramatic, ask the police to park a squad car in front of the library or even turn on the sirens during a strategic moment of the production. If you have funding, hire a local troupe to scale down their production to a teen-appropriate library setting.

- Read *Sisterhood of the Traveling Pants* as a group, and then let the girls decorate their own pair of jeans. Pick up beads, fabric paint, and other materials from a hobby store (or ask for donations). Hang the finished products in the teen area for a couple weeks as an eye-catching and colorful display of creativity.

- Coordinate a slumber party or lock-in. This will require some enthusiastic staff and parent volunteers who are willing and able to endure a nearly sleepless night. The trade-off is an excellent opportunity to bond with participants. Plan lots of activities such as trivia, scavenger hunts, food bars, and door prizes. Schedule it near the start of your summer reading club and recruit teens to help decorate YA and children's areas, allowing the evening to serve a practical purpose in addition to being fun.

Books and Authors

- Partnering with schools, sponsor a "meet the author" event. Ask participants to read a select number of books from a list. Prepare this list by doing (or delegating!) a little research on which authors might be available during a specific time period (find their Web sites and e-mail agents or publishers). Afterward, have them vote on which author they would like to invite. Be sure to inform the media of this program well in advance.

- Some of the most rewarding programs are book discussion groups. Recruit some reliable people whom you know will show up from week to week to be your core group. Make flyers and advertise that you will have snacks during the first planning meeting. Let the kids decide on the list of books they would like to read and discuss. Let them also decide when to meet.

- Obtain school reading lists and start a book discussion group based on novels the students have to read, anyway. Work out an extra credit deal for participants.

- One look at the multitude of mother-daughter adolescent survival books available makes it clear that this can be painful and terrible time for that special relationship. Host mother-daughter book discussion groups to give moms and girls an opportunity to spend quality time and maybe learn something new about one another.

- Do not exclude the boys! Studies show that relationships between young teen boys and their moms are significantly better than that of girls (Fenwick 1994). Perpetuate that nice bond by pioneering a mother-son book group as well. Or try parent-child and hope to recruit some dads.

- Ask young adolescents to submit book reviews for a simple prize— something as simple as a full-sized candy bar has appeal. Tie this into a special event such as *Teen Read Week* or during the school's holiday break. Post these on a bulletin board, on your Web site or blog. Create forms that are quick and easy for participants to fill out: What did you like/dislike about the book? Who was your favorite character? Do you have a favorite scene?

- If your library is near an assisted living center, they may be amenable to intergenerational programming. Book groups are ideal, especially theme-based. Read books from certain eras or in specific genres. Look at *5-Star Programming and Services for Your 55+ Library Customers* (Mates 2003) and *Serving Seniors: A How-to-Do-It Manual for Librarians* (Honnold 2004) for ideas on pairing seniors with teens, as well as www.eldersong.com for resource ideas.

- Plan book discussions that will appeal specifically to favorite themes of boys, such as horror, fantasy, or science fiction. First schedule a planning meeting so that they may take the lead in creating a reading list. On special nights, watch the movie version of the book or play networked games with literary tie-ins.

- Center book discussion groups on a specific series: *Left Behind*, *Cirque du Freak*, *Redwall*, *Keys to the Kingdom*. You are sure to find tips on publisher and author Web sites—puzzles, trivia, sample questions, and even craft activities. Or have hard-core fans brainstorm and devise their own book-related activities.

- Invite teens to participate in a traditional children's program such as a Caldecott voting contest.

- Paperback book swaps can be very popular. You, the programmer, collect good donations throughout the year and start an initial pile with them. Even better, acquire advanced reading copies from local bookstores since they will be a hot commodity. Participants then bring their own books to put them out on tables. Count those paperbacks and give the kid that number of vouchers. For every book a kid brings, he may take an equal number home. This is an informal way for you to chat with teens about what they read. Plus, they may make new friends with similar literary interests. This does not necessarily have to be limited to books. Ask participants if they would be amenable to branching out to music CDs, electronic games, old VHS tapes, and DVDs.

- Transform the library into a coffeehouse. Brew a large pot, set out teas and hot water. Get some baked goods as well as the usual salty and sweet snacks. Cover the tables in your meeting room with colorful paper cloths and sprinkle magnetic poetry on top. Spread markers around for impromptu doodling and light candles. Play soft jazz. After you have heavily advertised this to the English teachers and library media specialists, host a poetry cafe, slam, or open mike. Display poetry books, especially for those who spontaneously decide to pick one up for a read aloud. Experiment with different themes for your coffeehouses: romance, politics, contemporary, retro. Make one night a Battle of the Bands (or solo musicians) or even Battle of the Bards, during which teens with a theatrical flair compete against one another by reading poems to the crowd.

Movies

- Get a license from http://www.movlic.com/library.html to show films at the library. Or avoid paying a licensing fee and explore the catalog of www.retrofilm.com. What theme nights would entice the teens? Horror or sci-fi during October? Romance in February? Old John Hughes faves for back-to-school September? Holiday classics, old and new, during November and December? Put film ratings on your advertisement to avoid inevitable questions from parents—stick to only G, PG, or PG-13 rated flicks.

- Find movie ideas on Rotten Tomatoes (http://www.rottentomatoes.com) and Movie Review Query Engine (http://www.mrqe.com/lookup).

- Have a *Harry Potter*, *Star Wars*, or *Lord of the Rings* marathon weekend and encourage kids to dress in costume. Offer prizes for various "best of" categories. Pause the DVD player during key scenes so that actors in the audience can re-create the moment themselves.

- Get a group together to play a product from the *Scene-It* series, movie or TV trivia that combines traditional board games with DVD clips (www.sceneit.com).

- Read the book/watch the movie clubs are entertaining. Check out http://movies.yahoo.com/mv/upcoming/bygenre/basedonabook/2004 for a list of ideas. Besides *Harry Potter* and *Lord of the Rings*, try *Holes*, *Because of Winn Dixie*, *Freaky Friday*, *Princess Diaries*, *Sisterhood of the Traveling Pants*, and *The Series of Unfortunate Events*.

- Partner with your local arts council to sponsor a filmmaker festival. Ask the newspaper's film critic to sit on the jury and write up the event in her next column. Make note of these creative participants, since you might be able to use them to create a promo piece on library happenings in the future.

- Ask someone from the local costume shop to teach kids how to do movie makeup, especially the scary kind. Once everyone is appropriately adorned, watch some seasonal flicks such as *Night of the Living Dead* or *Little Shop of Horrors*. Serve gross food (eyeballs, bloody fingers, etc.) of course!

Anime

- Many comic stores host sessions on comic collecting and drawing. Approach one in your area and ask if they can bring a workshop to the library.

- Host an anime festival and show movies, display your collection, and have an artist on-hand for drawing advice. Find films ideas at www.comics2film.com. Check out this excellent article for ideas on showing anime in the library: http://pdfs.voya.com/An/ime/Anime.pdf.

- Sponsor a club for anime fans, something that will certainly attract the boys and hopefully their companions as well. Watch episodes of anime and then encourage them to draw. Let them swap books and ideas with each other and browse the new magazines that have arrived at the branch. If you can recruit a teen advisory group member to run the show, this may be a very low-maintenance activity for staff.

Games

- Stock your teen area with games that will be guaranteed to be used after school and on weekends. For $200 from the library Friends group, you can go on a shopping spree! A list of just a few includes *Risk, Monopoly, Scrabble, Clue, Cranium, Trivial Pursuit* (with updated cards), *Uno*, playing cards, *Pictionary, Jenga, Life, Balderdash, Sorry, Taboo, Yahtzee, Outburst,* chess, and checkers. Do not forget TV tie-in games such as *Jeopardy* and *Wheel of Fortune*.

- Host role-playing game days such as playing *Magic: The Gathering* or *Dungeons & Dragons*. Sponsor regular nights for participants to gather and play, with snacks.

- Do you have a computer lab or enough terminals side by side? Stay after hours once a month for a multiplayer online gaming night. Let teens play *RuneScape* (a fantasy world in which developed characters interact by talking, trading, exploring, and battling) or *Halo* (a science fiction world with combat-oriented play). This gives teens the chance to shout about their characters without being shushed, and gather round the terminals without being limited to two per station. Order in some pizzas and soda. Find other game suggestions at blizzard.com.

- Look for Linda W. Braun's *VOYA* article (2004, p. 189) on the importance of acknowledging the place of electronic gaming in the lives of teens. Create programs around this, such as discussions and demonstrations of popular games, how to search the Internet for cheat codes, or inviting a game designer as guest speaker. Join the LibGaming discussion group for discussions and ideas (http://groups-beta.google.com/group/LibGaming).

- If your meeting room is large, or you have ample lawn space, try a live chess game. Create the squares from poster board and ask each team to designate themselves by wearing a specific T-shirt or hat. Recruit the school's chess club advisor, or even a teen expert, to moderate.

Celebrations

- What ethnic groups comprise your population? Host events to honor Cinco de Mayo, Los Posadas, Black History Month, Italian Saints Day, Chinese New Year, St. Lucia's Day, Kwanzaa, or whatever people celebrate in your area. Food, readings from appropriate literature, crafts, art contests, and displays are all fitting. Use Yahooligans to search each holiday and find many resources.

- Check *Chase's Annual Events* or *The World Almanac* (subscribe to its monthly e-mail newsletter at www.worldalmanac.com) for other occasions to honor, including Elvis Presley's birthday on January 7, National TV Turnoff Week in late April, National Hamburger Month in May, National Candy Month in June, the premiere of MTV in August (1981), and World Vegetarian Day on October 1. The possibilities are endless, and you can tailor the celebrations to the needs and interests of your specific community.

• Center a spiritual exploration around Halloween. Offer tarot card readings, palmistry, and a demo of some easy yoga techniques. Do not forget to pass around the magic eight ball! Serve gross food or snacks that are all orange and black.

Is the Super Bowl coming up? Get hold of a play station and one of the popular football games. Hook it up to the projection screen in your meeting room and let the kids take turns. Serve typical Super Bowl munchies, bought in bulk at Sam's Club. Have another TV (or two) running in the corners of the room, playing the actual game.

TEEN ADVISORY BOARDS

If you are lucky to have a group of dedicated youth who sincerely want to be involved in program planning, let them assist! A Teen Advisory Board (TAB), otherwise known as a Teen Advisory Group (TAG), can be your most valuable source of ideas and legwork. Participants are given the opportunity to make a real impact in the community. They can earn volunteer credits and make valuable use of their time. Let the service organizations and honor societies at local middle schools know that you are recruiting. The TAB may be the first chance for a young teen to be involved in a group separate from parents or school in which their voice is truly heard. Rely on them for any of the following aspects of programming: brainstorming ideas, creating advertising, hanging flyers, word-of-mouth promotion, setting up rooms, putting together displays, hosting or helping with crowd control during events, and soliciting audience evaluations. YALSA offers helpful resources about TABs on its Web site http:// www.ala.org/ala/yalsa/tags/tags.htm. Join an electronic discussion group on this topic: YA-YAAC (http://lp-web.ala.org:8000/guest/listutil/YA-YAAC).

While many young adolescents have as little time as adults with all of their school and extracurricular activities, it may be unrealistic for your TAB to be completely involved in program planning. But YALSA's Teen Read Week (TRW) is another matter. The TRW, described on ALA's site www.ala.org/yalsa, is an annual week-long program boosted by a different theme and amazing graphics each year. It is an opportunity to promote the library with a big splash.

Programs relating to this week can become a project for which your TAB takes ownership. They can set goals, prioritize the goals, and work toward them for months. Have them consider how their library's TRW should be publicized and what promotional materials they would like the library to purchase from ALA. When should a special program be held, and what day and time will maximize attendance? Recruit the TAB to help with children's programs by taking tickets, decorating, and crowd control. Have them participate in reader's theater or monitor craft workshops. Ask them to dress in costume for theme-based events.

NUTS AND BOLTS OF PLANNING PROGRAMS

Organization

Someone should be the overall program coordinator. The person assigned to this task should be the point person for finding, contacting, and narrowing down details with the presenter; getting the paperwork rolling; requesting promotional materials and media plugs; ensuring payment for the performer; and gathering data on audience attendance and patron evaluations. Some library systems are highly structured and most plan their events months in advance; others can be more spontaneous. You must, of course, work within your system, but you do not have to do it alone. In addition, many other tasks are required for the production of the program—room setup, material displays, gathering necessary supplies or snacks, greeting the presenter, and monitoring the program. All of this may be delegated to other staff or volunteers. An excellent resource on program planning from start to finish is *Adult Programs in the Library* (Lear 2002). Despite its title, the process of program development described may be applied to any age group.

Mailing lists are invaluable. Post a question and you will get tons of feedback, including specific Web sites for ideas. Try YALSA-BK (http://lp-web.ala.org:8000/guest/info/YALSA-BK) for discussion of teen literature and the logistics of YA services, PUBYAC (send the message "subscribe pubyac" to listproc@prairienet.org) for general chat with those who work with children and young adolescents, and TAGAD-L (send an e-mail to tagad-l-subscribe@topica.com) for practical program ideas.

Money

Funding may come from an overall budget, donations, or a foundation. A programming budget does not have to be large. Many community libraries get by on limited funds. Creativity is your only boundary. If funds are low, volunteerism and community partnerships are key. Local merchants may be willing to donate craft materials, prizes, and snacks. Make the rounds to talk to them in person, or do a mass solicitation mailing on your library's letterhead. Often, Friends of the Library groups are a source of revenue, so recruit your TAB to help out with that all-important biannual book sale and other fund-raisers.

Certainly, money drives the number of events that your library may offer, but programming is possible despite a small budget size. Responses from a listserv survey on successful programs for young adolescents varied greatly. Some worked with $6,000 annually for a single branch, and others relied on gifts from their Friends group. Nearly all respondents credited the efforts of teen volunteers or organized TABs with the success of programs. Examples of winning happenings included the following:

- A small town library that shares teen funds with the children's department hosts monthly middle school book groups (with donated snacks), a babysitting certification class, a mural workshop to decorate blank wall space in the building, a girls-only writers group, and programs facilitated by local comic artists and writers.

- A suburban library that receives $3,000 annually from Friends hosts one program per week during the summer, one during TRW, and two during the school year. Most popular are gaming nights and Yu-Gi-Oh gatherings.

- A central library situated in a bustling civic center is able to offer several programs per month during the school year, in addition to those during summer. Knitting, mendhi tattoing, an urban legends storyteller, and a human board game have been well attended. They also partner with local arts centers for 'zine workshops and talks from established artists.

- With $7,000 per year to fund programming, one urban system schedules monthly Saturday afternoon events. These include watching *Harry Potter*, followed by a trivia contest and creating care packages for soldiers overseas.

- A library in an affluent suburban system has partnered with dance and karate studios as well as its public schools for programming. In addition to poetry cafes, crafty events such as candle making, knitting, and scrapbooking were hits.

- One library plans programs till their money runs out. With attendance of mainly 11- to 14-year-olds, successes included game days (with video games projected onto a big screen), movie screenings after hours, tie dyeing, and a monthly book club.

- With an annual budget of $2,600, one system plans three programs per month during the school year, one during TRW and one per week during summer. They have had a pumpkin carving and painting contest (with prizes), a Shakespeare acting workshop, and a scary movie marathon. Collaborating with a local coffeehouse resulted in a poetry slam.

Timing

Look at the community calendar to figure out the best opportunities for programming. Do lots of youth stick around the neighborhood for spring break, or are they all off on trips? Is your library busy on the weekend, or do Monday nights tend to attract the most patrons? Since young adolescents are not yet driving, their parents or older siblings may be more apt to drop them off for an evening program rather than trying to get them to the library after school and compete with sports, lessons, and church groups. Thursdays seem to be the least heavy homework night. Or, Saturday mornings (not too early!) may be worth a try. Experiment with timing—offer a variety for a year and then do some statistical comparisons. What days and times generated the greatest attendance? What seasonal differences do you observe? During the summer, what times are they able to get rides to the library? Perhaps it might work to schedule several programs on one day rather than spread throughout the month. Being informed of your community and the activities of teens within it is crucial so that programs can be scheduled during the best no-conflict times possible. It may be advantageous to collaborate with agencies such as schools or recreation centers so that large groups already there may join in your activities.

Defining the Audience

Unless the program specifically asks for parental involvement, do not allow parents to observe. This puts a damper on the mood, especially during creative programs such as poetry readings or book discussions. You are offering a safe place for youth to interact and must be firm on not allowing adults to mar the atmosphere. If you offer tickets, stress that they are for the youth participants only. Encourage parents to browse your great collection while they wait for the program to end, or suggest that parents simply drop off participants at the library, depending on your unattended minor policy. The same goes for older teens or children who want to attend your appealing programs. You do not want to compromise the integrity of this 'tween-only space by allowing other age groups in. The more you develop the reputation that your programs are just for them, the more young adolescents will encourage their friends to join in.

Atmosphere

No matter the size of your space, spruce it up. Play music before and after the program. Display any materials, in any format, that are related to the topic. Set out library brochures, booklists, and newsletter. Ask teen volunteers to greet the audience, so that they do not have to enter the room alone. Create atmospheres to fit your program theme: candles for poetry cafes, dim lights for Halloween events, disco balls for music performances or open mics. Alter the meeting room with posters, streamers, and tablecloths so that the space is transformed for each event.

Assessment

Do not forget evaluations. Keep them simple: how do you rate the program on a scale of 1–10? What did you like best or least? What other programs would you like the library to offer? Keep records of programs by creating a database to track specific performers, the days and times offered, staff and patron comments, cost, what worked and what did not, and notes for future events. Offer paper evaluations to the audience and enter their comments into the database. You may also want to ask how they heard about the program to determine which publicity materials were effective. How did display materials circulate after the program? Record your, and other staff's, observations as much as those of patrons. One word of caution: never compare your program for young adolescents to that of the children's department. That is simply not realistic. Since young adolescents can choose to attend your program the numbers will be fewer, while children's puppet and magic shows are almost always guaranteed a full house. Consider any participation at a program for teens, of any age, a success. Teens have a lot going on, including extracurricular activities and parents who are not always accustomed to bringing them to library for a special circumstance. Also, a big audience is not always desirable. Many programs will have to be limited—arts and crafts or anything involving extensive giveaways. You need to weigh the benefits of quality versus quantity. With all programs, do not forget to set up display tables of materials. And be sure to write thank you notes to all performers and presenters.

CONCLUSION

While initially intimidating, programming is lots of fun. Once you have got the logistics worked out, creative ideas will begin to flow. The library can and should be much more than a homework center for teens transitioning out of the children's room. You will quickly see the rewards in planning special events for young teens during this particularly awkward time of life. The energy that abounds in young teens is addictive—involve them in your activities and make your library a bona fide hangout for these most valuable patrons.

WORKS CITED

Braun, Linda W. "What's in a Game?" *VOYA* 27, no. 3 (2004): 189.

Chelton, Mary K. "YA Programming Roundup." *Top of the News* 1 (November 1975): 43.

Fenwick, Elizabeth. *Adolescence: The Survival Guide for Parents and Teenagers*. London: Dorling Kindersley, 1994.

Honnold, RoseMary. *Serving Seniors: A How-to-Do-It Manual for Librarians*. New York: Neal-Schuman, 2004.

Jones, Patrick, Michele Gorman, and Tricia Suellentrop. *Connecting Young Adults and Libraries*, 3rd ed. New York: Neal-Schuman, 2004.

Lear, Brett. *Adult Programs in the Library*. Chicago: American Library Association, 2002.

Mates, Barbara T. *5-Star Programming and Services for Your 55+ Library Customers*. Chicago: American Library Association, 2003.

Meyers, E. "The Coolness Factor: Ten Libraries Listen to Youth." *American Libraries* 30, no. 10 (November 1999): 42–45.

Porter, Cheryl. *Gross Grub: Retch-Ed Recipes That Taste Heavenly but Look Like Heck*. New York: Random House, 1995.

Rogers, JoAnn V. *Libraries and Young Adults: Media Services and Librarianship*. Littleton, CO: Libraries Unlimited, 1979.

Schiedermayer, Ellie. *Got Tape?* Iola, WI: Krause Publications, 2002.

Wenger, Jennifer. *Teen Knitting Club: Chill Out and Knit*. New York: Artisan, 2004.

Wilson, Joe. *Ductigami: The Art of the Tape*. Erin, ON: Boston Mills Press, 1999.

FOR FURTHER READING

Chelton, Mary K. *Excellence in Library Services to Young Adults: The Nation's Top Programs*, 3rd ed. Chicago: American Library Association, 2000.

Dickerson, Constance B. *Teen Book Discussion Groups @ the Library*. New York: Neal-Schuman, 2004.

Edwards, Kirsten. *Teen Library Events: A Month-by-Month Guide*. Westport, CT: Greenwood Press, 2002.

Gillespie, Kellie M. *Teen Volunteer Services in Libraries*. Lanham, MD: Scarecrow Press, 2004.

Honnold, Rosemary. *More Teen Programs That Work*. New York: Neal-Schuman, 2005.

———. *101+ Teen Programs That Work*. New York: Neal-Schuman, 2003.

Ishizuka, Kathy. "Study: Don't Underestimate Youth Programs." *School Library Journal* 51, no. 3 (March 2005): 22.

Kan, Katharine. *Sizzling Summer Reading Program for Young Adults*, 2nd ed. Chicago: American Library Association, 2006.

Long, Sarah Ann. "Two Afterschool Programs ASPIRE to Take the Initiative." *American Libraries*. 31, no. 3 (March 2000): 7.

Nichols, C. Allen, ed. *Thinking Outside the Book: Alternatives for Today's Teen Library Collections*. Westport, CT: Libraries Unlimited, 2005.

Ott, Valerie. *Teen Programs with Punch: A Month-by-Month Guide*. Westport, CT: Libraries Unlimited, 2006.

Reid, Rob. *Something Funny Happened at the Library: How to Create Humorous Programs for Children and Young Adults*. Chicago: American Library Association, 2003.

Rutherford, Dawn, and Brenna Shanks. "A Fantastic Team: School and Public Libraries." *Voice of Youth Advocates* 27, no. 5 (December 2004): 358–359.

Tuccillo, Diane P. *Library Teen Advisory Groups*. Lanham, MD: Scarecrow Press, 2004.

Vaillancourt, Renee. *Excellence in Library Services to Young Adults: The Nation's Top Programs*, 4th ed. Chicago: American Library Association, 2004.

Wilson-Lingbloom, Evie. *Hangin' Out at Rocky Creek: A Melodrama in Basic Young Adult Services in Public Libraries*. Metuchen, NJ: Scarecrow Press, 1994.

5

"I Want to Read That Book!" Booktalking to 'Tweens and Young Teens

Kristine Mahood

Booktalking blasts open the covers of books and shows teens what they can experience through reading. For avid teen readers, booktalking reinforces their love of reading and books by showing them even more books to read. For occasional readers, booktalking reminds them that books can be fun, exciting, thought provoking, and emotionally satisfying. For reluctant readers, booktalking can re-inspire them to give books another chance. And when I refer to "booktalking," I mean not only the crazy-for-books energy radiating from young adult librarians, but also the energy generated by teen audiences. Teens are listening. They are reacting to plot twists and jokes. They are asking questions. And when librarians conclude their booktalk programs by asking teens to talk about good books they would recommend, teens' crazy-for-books energy bursts out. Even the most resistant readers can see how much books can offer teens: fun, excitement, deep emotions, wonder, and mind-expanding answers to big questions. Back when they were young children, teens enjoyed storytimes and listened to books read out loud by parents and other adults. As older children, they first read books chosen for them by parents and teachers, and then as 'tweens started to choose their own books. Entering middle school, younger teens are choosing virtually all of their own books. At the same time, they are expected to read more textbooks and other assigned books than they did in elementary school. By showcasing fiction and personal interest nonfiction, young adult librarians send the message that reading is not just for school, it is also for personal enjoyment and knowledge. And by booktalking a wide variety of books, librarians show that people read different types of books in order to enjoy different types of reading experiences. Books as various as mysteries, realistic novels, lavishly illustrated popular science books, self-help manuals, teen poetry collections, and graphic novels meet teens' disparate reading needs: to enjoy stories, to learn facts, and to follow critical arguments in book genres such as poetry, self-help, or weird popular science. And by booktalking books that appeal to a variety of reading interests, young adult librarians also help teens to continue developing their reading skills.

Presenting booktalk programs also allows young adult librarians to promote the public library by talking about reference and reader advisory services, Internet and word processing access, and teen activities and events. Describing the teen space at their library, young adult librarians are telling younger teens that there is a place they can go to in between school and home, where they can get what they need, meet up with friends, and relax. By asking teens for their recommendations about books to read, young adult librarians demonstrate that teens have expertise to contribute.

This chapter will begin by exploring why it is so much fun to booktalk to younger teens. Next, we will examine teen reading interests, and insights into the appeal of books. I will briefly review connecting with schools, taking care of yourself as a booktalker, planning "special effects," and setting the stage for a booktalk presentation. The chapter concludes with a sample booktalk program, which includes booktalks; remarks about library collections, services, and events; and book recommendations by teens.

WHY IT IS SO MUCH FUN TO BOOKTALK TO YOUNG TEENS

Booktalking to 'tweens and young teens is a blast! Why? Because! Because teen brains are growing, and they are hungry for stories and facts. Because, in order to develop reading skills, teens need to read a wide variety of books, and as a booktalker it is fun to talk about a variety of books. Because younger teens' lives are growing, too, and their greater experiences and understanding mean that they appreciate a variety of books. And because teens can be incredibly welcoming and appreciative.

For many years, scientists thought that the majority of brain growth took place during early childhood. Recent studies using magnetic resonance imaging have revealed otherwise. Researchers such as Dr. Jay Giedd have shown that during puberty and early adolescence, the human brain's gray matter undergoes a tremendous growth spurt, producing huge numbers of new brain cells and the dendrites that facilitate communication between neurons (Strauch 2003, p. 17). Giedd and other researchers describe the teenage brain as exuberant with growth. Every area of the brain is growing, and the frontal lobes—the locus of impulse control and planning—reach their peak growth in girls at age eleven and in boys at age twelve (Strauch 2003, p. 16). Then the brain begins a process of reorganization, establishing synaptic connections and "pruning" for efficient operation. This time of brain boom and restructuring coincides with such observable teen behaviors as rampant curiosity, lack of inhibition about asking questions, and burgeoning interest in themselves, each other, crafts, hobbies, sports, music, you name it. Younger teens are discovering the world, and they have not yet decided what they like, so they are open to a lot of things. They are beginning to experience peer pressure, and nobody wants to be thought of as a dork, but if they have a question about a book, they are not going to censor themselves out of fear of not appearing cool, restrained, and calmly adult. No, they will *ask*.

Not only are younger teens' interests expanding exponentially, but they also enjoy looking at things in new ways. They are discovering humor, skepticism, and irony. As children, they devoured riddle and joke books. They grew up watching "The Simpsons," and now they are reading *Mad* magazine. And as anybody knows who has spent any time at all with younger teens, they are always ready to fall down laughing. All of this means that young adult librarians can and should display and booktalk a variety of books—fiction and nonfiction—written in a wide variety of styles, from serious to hilarious. Librarians can booktalk these books in a range of presentation styles, too, and in voices that range from flat deadpan to high-pitched funny. It is wide open.

Not only are younger teens' brains expanding, but their lives are expanding, too, beyond home, next door, and the neighborhood elementary school. As children, they looked on as their older brothers and sisters wrestled with teen issues. Now those issues are theirs. Younger teens are more likely than children to assume responsibilities at home: for younger siblings, for cleaning and laundry, and for yard work. Their friends used to be the kids next door, and their classmates inhabited just one elementary school classroom. Now they are meeting many more teens from other schools. Their elementary teacher taught every subject and was a constant—and reassuring—presence. Now they have six teachers to fathom, and possibly a coach, band leader, and after-school activity advisor. At home and at school, teens are participating in discussions about social issues, from recycling to drug abuse. All of this means that their frame of reference is opening up, and with it, their curiosity and receptivity to new ideas and knowledge.

Younger teens' brains, interests, and lives are expanding, and publishers are meeting these expanded interests by offering a dazzling array of books. Adventure, fantasy, mystery, and other popular fiction genres pique teens' imagination, while the recognizable characters and issue-driven plots explored by realistic fiction touch their hearts. They are watching anime cartoons on TV, and reading manga series as well as superhero comics and graphic novels. Nonfiction books are catching up to magazines in the variety of topics they cover, to meet teens' growing personal interests and informational needs.

Stoking younger teens' curiosity with books is a critical element in the development of their reading ability and enjoyment. In recent years, educational policies and financial resources have been devoted to improving reading instruction in elementary schools (Manzo 2004, p. 10). The dedication of schools, families, public libraries, and other literacy efforts has paid off: American fourth graders are scoring well on reading achievement tests (Clinton 2002, L5). Many older children's reading skills allow them to progress from easy readers to juvenile fiction, from basic nonfiction books to textbooks. As noted in "Adolescent Literacy: A Position Statement," when older children enter middle school, the focus of the curriculum generally changes from developing reading and math skills, to using those skills to master subject content (Moore 1999, p. 101). Any ongoing responsibility for teaching younger teens how to read well is given to English teachers, who are also expected to teach content (Moore 1999, p. 101). Ideally, reading skills continue to develop through grades four through eight, as children and young teens gain vocabulary and learn how to read some books for facts, some for opinions, and some for enjoyment (Chall 1983, p. 22). As older children, they were so beguiled by books that they willingly lost themselves in fantastic adventures and other stories (Donelson and Nilsen 1997, p. 40). As younger teens, readers are finding themselves in stories, devouring novels about teen life and biographies about real lives (Donelson and Nilsen 1997, p. 41). As sixth, seventh, and eighth graders, younger teens are primed for reading to lift off from the printed words on the page and soar into their brains and hearts, alongside their curiosity about themselves and the world and the emotions stirred up by their sense of discovery and wonder. Moreover, as twenty-first-century adults, younger teens will need highly developed literacy skills to understand and use the information that affects their employment, financial, medical, political, and personal lives (Moore 1999, p. 99).

Studies of teen reading have continued since "Adolescent Literacy: A Position Statement" appeared in 1999. Just as research in previous decades identified an achievement gap between girls and boys in math and science, with recommendations for remedies, so also have educational professionals turned their attention to differences in reading. Research has confirmed what boys, parents, teachers, and librarians have long observed. On average, it takes boys longer to learn to read and to develop as readers; they read less than girls, and they are more likely to read nonfiction than girls (Jones 2005, p. 37). Moreover, when boys' reading interests in humor, science fiction, fantasy, hobbies, and sports are at variance with the focus of English and Language Arts curricula, the disconnect widens (Jones 2005, p. 37).

The needs of all teen readers are explored in "Reading Next: A Vision for Action and Research in Middle and High School Literacy," a report issued in late 2004 by the Carnegie Corporation of New York and the Alliance for

Excellent Education. According to its findings, an estimated 8 million young people in grades four through twelve struggle through reading and writing (Biancarosa and Snow 2004, p. 7). The report urges schools to work with teens using methods such as comprehension instruction, tutoring, collaborative learning centered on texts, writing, giving more schooltime to reading, testing, and motivation (Biancarosa and Snow 2004, pp. 4–5).

Motivation is what young adult librarians can bring to the effort to keep younger teens on an upward reading trajectory. To find out what types of books teens like to read, young adult librarians can talk with teens, teachers, school librarians, and public library staff. Working from their knowledge of popular fiction genres, realistic fiction themes, and nonfiction topics, young adult librarians can motivate teens to read by booktalking books that satisfy those interests, while throwing in some different types of books to pique teens' curiosity.

It is sometimes a challenge to booktalk to a classroom of younger teens juiced by hormones and social hyper-awareness, bouncing around like water drops in a hot skillet. And yet it is that very liveliness that can inspire young adult librarians to give booktalk performances that are wide ranging, spontaneous, and sometimes just a tiny bit out of control. As a young adult librarian, you have helped younger teens find books they would like to read. Booktalking is your opportunity to bring what you have learned from one-on-one readers' advisory to a larger audience. Audiences of adults can be polite, audiences of older teens can be calm, but younger teens are right out there. They are eager to get it, get it, get it. They will ask questions. They will interrupt. They will gasp. They will laugh. And they will come up to you afterward, pick up the books, ask you questions, and be amazed that yes, you have read all those books—and more. They will ask you, how did you know what to say about the books? They will tell you about more books they have read and liked. They will thank you for coming to their class—and you will hardly be able to wait until you can come back.

SOMETHING FOR EVERYONE

What is one of the most—if not the most—valuable commodities today? Time.

As they emerge from childhood, younger teens experience increasing demands on their time. When they were children, they could get up in the morning, throw on their clothes, and be ready for school. Now they spend more time bathing, grooming, dressing, checking their backpacks for assignments, and assembling musical instruments or other paraphernalia. At school, they no longer stay in the same classroom with the same teacher, but rush from classroom to classroom, from gym to practice room, in a cacophony of noise and excitement, with a million details swirling around and demanding their attention. Home again, they may instant message friends for a while, before starting on chores and homework. They may be involved in sports, clubs, and other after-school activities. Or they may be hanging out at the library or an after-school center until 5:30 or 6:00 p.m. or later—whenever a parent or other adult can pick them up after work. On the weekends there are family responsibilities, more studying, and fun with friends.

There is a lot going on in teens' lives, and not a lot of time for reading. But if teens hear about books that sound good, they will make time.

READING INTERESTS

The best way to find out what 'tweens and younger teens are reading is to ask them. While a readers' advisory interview is a natural time to talk about books, there are additional ways to bring up the subject of reading and books, whether at the conclusion of reference assistance, or in casual conversation. "Reading anything good lately? What are you reading for fun these days? Can I ask, what's that book you're reading? Is it any good?" These are just a few of the ways you can ask younger teens about books.

Another way to find out what 'tweens and young teens are reading is to read book reviews written by teens, which appear on many public and school library teen services Web sites. You can also ask older children what they enjoy reading. Avid child readers tend to evolve into avid 'tween and teen readers, and the genres, themes, and topics of interest often remain the same in teen reading. Some of the books that 'tweens and younger teens enjoy will be catalogued as "juvenile" and others as "young adult." For example, juvenile and young adult fantasy fiction is rife with books—stand-alone titles or series—that tell complex stories teeming with well-developed characters and detailed descriptions. Find out from library colleagues what books older children, 'tweens, and younger teens are asking about and reading. Talk with elementary and middle school media specialists about what is flying off their shelves. Find out what is flying off *your* shelves, by looking at the children's and young adult books on shelving carts. To keep current with new books with children's/young adult crossover appeal, read reviews in library and educational journals of books grouped into the grades 5–8 category. Scan the children's books' best seller lists published by *Publisher's Weekly*. Your local newspaper may carry equivalent information collected by local or regional bookstores. Online bookstores such as Amazon.com and Barnesandnoble.com post lists of popular children's and teens' books. Keep in mind, however, that these lists represent only the most widely purchased books—by young people and their families on their behalf. Check the "best books" lists published by such review media as *VOYA* and *School Library Journal,* and library associations like the YALSA and the ALSC. What you are looking for is not simply particular titles, but also the genres, themes, and subject reading interests they represent.

Best seller and award winner lists offer useful information, but they do not tell the whole story of what teens are reading. Younger teens in your library are also devouring books that are neither best sellers nor award winners. Cast your net wide.

How Books Appeal to 'Tweens and Younger Teens

Teens choose books for many reasons. Perhaps they want to read a novel like the last book they enjoyed so much. Maybe they want something totally different. Maybe all of their friends are reading and talking about a particular book or series. They may need to know more about a topic, for personal or educational reasons. Many adults also choose books from personal interests or needs, or because of socially driven reasons such as relentless advertising, friend or family recommendations, celebrity promotions, or book group membership.

What is it about books that appeal to younger teens? Adult and young adult readers' advisory experts refer to the elements of books that readers enjoy as "appeal characteristics." Appeal characteristics are not necessarily the genres, themes, or subjects of books. Instead, they are the basic elements of fictional stories and nonfiction narratives that catch readers' interests and make them race through the pages (or linger over them). Appeal characteristics have been identified by adult readers' advisory experts Joyce Saricks and Nancy Pearl, and young adult readers' advisory expert Diana Tixier Herald. Saricks (2005, p. 40) refers to these elements as pacing, characterization, storyline, and frame. Nancy Pearl (2002, p. xi) dubs them story, character, setting, and language. Herald (2003, p. 5) focuses on teens' preferences for characters and strong plots—with a reminder that cool cover art helps, too. Because appeal characteristics transcend genre, theme, or subject, they allow readers to enjoy a variety of books (Saricks 2005). For example, teens who like funny situations and characters will often enjoy satiric science fiction, romantic comedy, or screwball stories of school life.

There are other elements in books that may appeal to teens, such as brevity. On the other hand, the popularity of fantasy novels and series by such authors as Cornelia Funke, Tamora Pierce, J. K. Rowling, Darren Shan, Jonathan Stroud, and J.R.R. Tokien testifies to the appeal of long books that pull their readers into created worlds. Teens may also identify elements they do not like in books, such as too much description or humor that is so heavy-handed it falls flat.

What follows are descriptions of four appeal characteristics—story, characters, setting, and language—with some suggestions on how to highlight these characteristics in booktalks.

Story

Many teens enjoy novels driven by fast-moving plots (Herald 2003, p. 5). Lots of action and dialogue and minimal description keep the pages turning. Adventure, mystery, suspense, horror, fantasy, and science fiction novels are fiction genres that offer story appeal. These books often begin with a "what if . . . ?" premise, and then run with it. Characters are sketched in quickly: it is usually sufficient that they are "regular" teens without complicated personal problems, with whom the majority of teens can rapidly identify. These teen heroes and heroines need to save the world, and do not have time for teen angst, family problems, troubled friends, bullies at school, and so on. They are too busy hurling from one plot crisis to the next to indulge in protracted ruminations about themselves, their relationships, or philosophical issues. They have to keep moving. Speed is not the only definition of a book with story appeal, however. Many mystery, suspense, and horror novels work their magic through a slow, creeping pace, revealing detail after detail as each page is turned. In fact, the slower pace allows for more character development—because there is more time built into the plot for the characters to think about what is happening, in addition to reacting to it.

The "what if . . . ?" premise also works well in the "truth is stranger than fiction" type of nonfiction exemplified by such popular science titles as *Fossil Fish Found Alive: Discovering the Coelacanth* (Walker 2002), the true story of the discovery of a fish species that survived dinosaur-era extinction.

To write booktalks with story appeal, set the scene, introduce the characters, and then get the plot in motion—fast. Bring the characters to their first plot challenge, let them surmount it, and then throw another obstacle in their path. Your booktalk shows that teens have what it takes to assess and solve problems, and to regroup when thwarted.

Character

Teens like reading books featuring characters and real-life people who, like themselves, are meeting the challenges of adolescent life (Herald 2003, p. 5). Like their teen readers, teen characters are figuring out how to be themselves, how to fit in, and how to sustain relationships with family members, friends, and other people. In books with character appeal, actions do not just happen; they are examined, turned over, and pondered for their significance. Readers like spending time with characters and getting to know them. In the case of some book series or books with sequels, readers look forward to the next book with the same eagerness as they bring to meeting up with friends.

And speaking of friends, teens' primary relationships are still with their parents and siblings, but friendship offers possibilities that are new and exciting, although sometimes disturbing or traumatic. Moving from elementary school to middle school, teens may experience rejection for the first time, as their longtime elementary school friends meet new people from other schools and drift out of their lives. Similarly, teens may meet new people from other schools who actively seek out their friendship rather than simply tolerating their presence due to neighborhood or single-classroom proximity. They are also plumbing romantic feelings, which run the gamut from one-sided crushes to tentative (or not-so-tentative) relationships. Friendships change, people change, and teens are finding out that establishing their individual identities and knowing how to relate to other people are major aspects of life. Teens are also finding out that some new friends are manipulative users.

While the third person narrative remains a major format, one of the hallmarks of fiction for teens is the first person narrative. First person narrative gives teen characters their voice, allowing them to talk directly to readers, seemingly independent of the adult author. Teen characters are also speaking to readers even more directly, through diaries, letters, and e-mail. And in nonfiction, teens are reaching other teens through their own poetry, autobiography, personal essays, and collections of self-help writing.

To write booktalks with character appeal, use the protagonist's name in the first sentence or two of your booktalk and repeat it throughout the booktalk. Quickly sketch in a description of the protagonist's appearance, personality, and situation. Use the names of one or two other characters throughout the booktalk. Hearing the characters' names bonds teen listeners with the characters, giving teens a stake in the story. Part of the appeal of characters is their age: teens prefer books with characters who are their age or a bit older (Herald 2003, p. 5). Work the characters' ages into booktalks by describing them as "12-year-old Jerry" or "15-year-old Greta," or referring to middle or high school settings. Younger teens like hearing that teens their age are the stars of exciting stories. They also like aspiring to the sophistication of 15-year-old characters.

Setting

When you ask a teen about the fantasy or science fiction novel he is reading, and he describes its author-created world in great detail, he is telling you that what appeals to him about the book is its setting. He may have outlined the plot or mentioned some of the characters. But what he talked about the most was the setting. Some younger teens enjoy books set in places they know well, such as their hometowns or the nearest big city. They may not live in the city, but they have visited it, and like to think they can easily imagine a story taking place there. Other younger teens enjoy reading books set in places they know little about, such as fantasy worlds—or a big city, a small town, a wilderness area, another country, or another time period. Suspense stories are often described in terms of their atmosphere, that is, a combination of physical setting and the characters' intellectual and emotional response to it.

Like adult readers who enjoy reading books set in familiar occupational settings, some younger teens enjoy reading stories that take place at school. School is where they spend a lot of time, where they meet their friends, and where they face academic, physical, and social challenges, failures, and triumphs. Funny stories depicting teens confounding or outwitting school bureaucrats are a staple of teen fiction, movies, and TV.

To write booktalks with setting appeal, describe the surroundings of a scene with just enough detail so that your audience feels grounded in an actual place, rather than floating in an indeterminate space. Once the action of the scene begins, teens will thus be able to imagine it. Include a few colors in descriptions of people and settings: brown eyes, pale skin, cinnamon skin, green eyes, blue sky, yellow sun, black sky, bright white moon, etc. Avoid using too many colors or overly long descriptions. With just a few brushstrokes, you can paint the scenery behind the action and dialogue.

Language

When adults rhapsodize about the way a book is written, what they are identifying as an appeal characteristic is language; that is, the author's mastery of expression. Traditional and contemporary classics, books chosen for reading by book groups, and other literary novels may feature compelling plots, complex characters, and evocative settings, but it is the author's "voice" that distinguishes them.

Teens are also responsive to masterful writing. When a teen describes a book as "so funny," quoting smart aleck dialogue and re-enacting scenes, she is telling you that what appeals to her about the book is the language. In fact, younger teens joke around with each other a lot, flexing their growing communication and social skills through humor. Thus, Mia's humorous take on things has made Meg Cabot's *Princess* series a runaway success. Burgeoning emotions draw teens to sad books, too, dealing with accidents, illnesses, and death. Characters share their feelings in narratives and dialogue that touch teens' hearts.

To write booktalks with language appeal, work the style of the book into the style of your booktalk. Write a booktalk for a funny book with sentences that tumble headlong over each other. Write a booktalk for a serious book by succinctly and indelibly conveying what the audience needs to know to get started, and then slow down the pace as you use words that cut to the bone of the characters' emotions, pulling the audience into the story. Repetition can be very effective. Repeat the same word, phrase, or sentence in between paragraphs, like the refrain of a song. Play with sound, tossing in two- or three-word rhymes, assonant rhymes, and alliteration. Rusty on rhyming? Warm up for booktalk writing by reading rhyming poetry out loud. Once those rhymes are rolling around in your head, you will hear more rhymes as you write.

Incorporating principles of readers' advisory into booktalking helps to promote reading and books to younger teens. By choosing books that exemplify different appeal characteristics, you can avoid falling into a monotonous pattern of booktalking nothing but story-driven books. By writing booktalks that highlight those characteristics, you can avoid falling into a monotonous pattern of booktalking every book in the same breathless, action-driven style.

TAKE CARE OF YOURSELF

Booktalking is mental work. Read your booktalks over and over. Some young adult librarians memorize their booktalks word for word. I concentrate on pounding the major appeal characteristics into my head: characters' names, plot twists, scene settings, and lines of dialogue. Then I recollect the book as a whole, so that my knowledge of the book is not confined to the booktalk that I wrote. Keeping a few extra details about the book in my head means that if I forget some detail of my written booktalk, I have something else I can weave in so I can continue the performance (Anderson and Mahood 2001, p. 107). These extra details also come in handy when, after delivering a booktalk a dozen or so times, I suddenly decide to revise it—in the middle of a school visit.

Booktalking is emotional work. It is not easy to stand up in front of a group and talk. What if you forget what you are going to say? What if they laugh? What if they just ignore you and talk among themselves? Relax:

- No audience wants a public speaker to fail, except for audiences made up of sadists and ideologues. It is just too cringe-inducing and embarrassing for everybody.

- Teachers and media school specialists usually prepare classes beforehand, reviewing what is and what is not acceptable behavior while listening to a guest speaker. They too want you to succeed, because, like them, you are promoting reading and books to teens. They typically intervene in case of distraction from the audience.

- Take heart from the fact that what you are doing is extremely important: promoting reading, books, and the public library to younger teens. Reading well is the key to educational success. In an information-driven society, reading well is the key to employment and career success, and to the mastery of financial, medical, political, and other realities.

- The books themselves are there to help you. Just holding the books in your hands can have a grounding effect. And remember, instead of talking entirely out of your head, you are telling a series of very short stories. You know you can make it from one story to the next.

- When you perform, you are not speaking as yourself, you are speaking as your professional young adult librarian persona. You are still yourself, only amped up a little. When you are "on," you are surrounded by an aura of energy.

Performing booktalks plunges you into intense distillations of action and emotion, as you deliver the essence of books. It can be mentally and emotionally taxing. So give your brain some breaks, by interspersing some quick show-and-tells about magazines and other library materials in between dramatic booktalks. Coast a little by explaining how to get a library card. Talk about upcoming teen events. Relax.

Booktalking is also physical work. An hour or a half hour before you are scheduled to speak, drink two or three cups water. This will get you hydrated and ready to speak. Drinking a lot of water is particularly helpful when booktalking early in the morning, as dehydration can set in overnight. Continue to drink water in between presentations, which will keep you hydrated. Bring cough drops or throat lozenges in case you need them. If you have a lunch break longer than the time it takes to eat lunch, go for a walk—outside, if possible. Breathe deeply, clear your mind, think about something else, and relax.

SPECIAL EFFECTS

Booktalk performance techniques that appeal to younger teen audiences include using facial expressions, body movements, vocal effects, and physical objects, or props. Used judiciously, these techniques can juice up booktalks. Used to excess, they can make you look like a fool who is desperate for laughs. Worse, they can make younger teen audiences feel as though they are being treated like little kids. Younger teens have discovered coolness, and can be ruthless in their dismissal of what they perceive of as uncool (even though they may secretly still like their childhood toys and enjoy watching cartoons).

With these caveats in mind, special effects can definitely bring more dimensions to booktalk performance. Facial expressions and body movements can be as straightforward as acting out what you are saying in your booktalk, such as leaning forward and squinting as you describe a character trying to see something. When a character suddenly realizes something, smack your forehead. In other words, illustrate your booktalk with your facial expression and body movements.

Vocal effects can also be fairly straightforward, like doing two different voices while pivoting from side to side, representing two characters talking to one another, and then leaning forward to the audience, representing the narrator. Microphones practically beg you to do sound effects, such as whistling winds, doors closing, footsteps tapping, etc. And then there is the fun of doing one character in a regular voice and another in a really funny voice. In *The Nose from Jupiter* (Scrimger 1998), eighth grader Alan reels when a bee flies into his nose. Only it is not a bee, it is a tiny spaceship flown by Norbert, who hails from Jupiter. Norbert's dialogue is helpfully printed in italics, making it easy to read aloud his lines in a high-pitched, out-of-breath voice.

Just as props facilitate the action on a stage set, so also can they lend verisimilitude to a booktalk. Hold up a running shoe and shrug. "Great shoes, but are they worth trying to steal? Luke asked himself that question, sitting in the interview room with the police who'd arrested him" (Coleman 2004). Bring makeup to illustrate books on makeup, pencils and drawing paper to accompany books on drawing manga, and a planning calendar when booktalking guidebooks on school success.

SETTING THE STAGE

A booktalk program is an opportunity to promote books to read, as well as the rest of what the public library has to offer. To connect with schools, contact the school media specialist. Ask if teachers would be interested in a program of fiction and nonfiction booktalks, with information about library collections, services, and events for teens. The program I offer is 35–40 minutes long, which fits into one standard class period. I suggest that two or three classes be combined and meet in the school library. How programs are scheduled is affected by the size of the school and the latitude that teachers are given to devote class time to presentations not directly related to instruction. In some schools, all of the Language Arts teachers jump on board, so you may be speaking to two or three classes per period, meeting in the school library. If you are speaking in a large space, request or bring a sound system so that you can speak in a natural tone of voice, rather than having to shout to be heard. School visits vary. In one small city located in my library district, the head librarian of the local library and I drive to three elementary schools in one day so that we can promote summer reading to sixth grade classes. In another location, one of the local library's youth services librarians and I visit a middle school over a two-day period so that we can present booktalks to all seventh and eighth grade English classes.

Follow up your phone contact with e-mail or a letter describing your program, including a list of the books you plan to booktalk. This will allow the school media specialist to create a display and to purchase books if necessary. Take advantage of this opportunity for you and the school media specialist to talk about books that are popular with teens at your respective locales. Both of you can also benefit from talking about books you have read and enjoyed, and from sharing ideas about promoting reading and books to teens.

It is easier for any audience to understand what you are talking about if they can see it, so when the school media specialist or teacher asks if you need any equipment, ask for a table to set up a display. If the school can provide you with tabletop display fixtures of various sizes, so much the better. Your display area, like a stage set, gives you a structured space in which to work with materials. Display fixtures facilitate promoting the variety and depth of materials available to younger teens at the public library. Bring book easels and brochure holders so that you can display your materials standing up and clearly visible, rather than stacking them on the table flat and unseen. Some books will warrant the full booktalk treatment. Other books will get quick shelf talks. And some materials you will simply hold up as show-and-tell examples of collections. When you arrive in the classroom, school library, or other program space, line up your large book easels in a back row and fill them with magazines and large nonfiction books. Fill up the brochure holders with such print promotions as booklists, bookmarks, library card applications, library service brochures, teen events brochures, and copies of the library's young adult newsletter (backed by cardboard or another surface, so they do not flop around). Line up the small book easels in a front row, staggering them so they do not block the view of the back row, and leave them empty. You will be filling them up as you booktalk. Bring handouts that include an annotated list of the books you are booktalking, plus such information as the library's Web site address, street address, phone number, business hours, and news of upcoming teen events. Stack your books in the order you plan to booktalk them, but leave a few out of the stack in case you need to substitute them in at the last minute.

SAMPLE BOOKTALK PROGRAM

This is the outline I typically follow for booktalk programs:

- Brief introduction
- Sudden Weirdness booktalks
- Introduction and program outline
- Realistic Fiction booktalks
- What you get with a library card
- Nonfiction booktalks
- Heart and Soul booktalks
- Upcoming teen events
- Always leave them laughing
- Let us all talk about books

For each section of the program, I describe what I say, and in most sections I directly quote what I say, indicated by quotation marks.

Sudden Weirdness Booktalk

After a brief introduction by the school media specialist or a teacher, I like to begin the program with a book that catapults a teen character out of an ordinary day and into an extraordinary situation. If no one has introduced me, I still like to start with a booktalk; I will introduce myself afterward. The idea is to jolt teens out of their regular classroom or library routine with their teacher or school media specialist, and into the booktalking zone with me. Good choices for Sudden Weirdness booktalks are science fiction, mysteries, and fantasy titles.

A Crack in the Line, by Michael Lawrence

Alaric's life stopped when Mum died in the train crash. It was two years ago, and nothing's been the same. Dad is distant. Neither Alaric nor Dad takes much care of the house, which is about one hundred years old. It's gray with dust and dirt, and practically falling down around their ears. Alaric can't see the point, really. Nothing will bring Mum back, so why bother?

Dad takes off on a business trip one snowy weekend, leaving Mum's sister, Aunt Liney, in charge.

"I don't need a babysitter," Alaric grumbles, but nobody pays any attention to him. He wanders off into the parlor, a cold, dark, dusty room nobody uses anymore. Alaric stares at a wooden carving of the house that Mum made, years ago. It stands under a dusty glass bell. When Alaric walks up to the carved house, he hears it humming. When he touches the glass, pain shoots through his hand up his arm, and he squeezes his eyes shut against the shock of it. Suddenly, his feet are freezing. He's standing outside, in the snow!

Brr, better get back inside the house. Not that he'll be much warmer: the furnace has been broken for weeks, and Alaric and Dad have been slowly freezing solid.

When Alaric gets back inside the house, he thinks he's come to the wrong place.

It's warm.

It's clean.

New carpets glow red and gold on the floor of the entrance hall. There's new-looking wallpaper, a mirror, and Alaric can smell flowers.

And strangest of all, a girl his age is standing there, staring at him.

"Who are you?" she asks.

"I'm Alaric," he answers. "Who are you, and what are you doing in my house?"

"I'm Naia," she answers. "Who are you, and what are you doing in *my* house?"

Alaric *is* in his house. But it's the house in the parallel reality where Mum and Dad had a daughter named Naia, Mum didn't die, and Naia is living the life that was taken away from Alaric. And Alaric wants it back.

Down the Rabbit Hole: An Echo Falls Mystery,
by Peter Abrahams

Like so many adventures in life, it all begins with a trip to the orthodontist.

Ingrid's at the orthodontist's, getting her braces adjusted. Which is about the most excitement she's had all week in Echo Falls, a quiet little town in the suburbs. Oh, right, Ingrid's also auditioning for the role of Alice in a production of "Alice in Wonderland" at the local theater. Wrestling with eighth-grade algebra homework definitely does not count in the excitement department. Anyway, Ingrid has all of her soccer gear with her, because she has to get to practice immediately after her orthodontist appointment. If she's late, she can't practice, and if she can't practice, the coach will make her warm the bench during their next game. Mom is supposed to pick Ingrid up and take her to practice, but she's late.

And getting later. Ingrid gives up and decides to walk to the soccer fields. She has a pretty good idea where they are. And how hard could it be to find the place? Echo Falls is a nice little town, right?

Ingrid gets lost almost immediately, and finds herself in a neighborhood she's never seen before. A door opens and a tall woman squints at her.

"You lost?" she asks, and offers to call Ingrid a cab.

Ingrid recognizes her. She's Cracked-Up Katie, the town eccentric. Katie invites Ingrid inside. Ingrid sits down, taking her red soccer cleats out of her gear bag so she can put them on before the cab arrives. Only Ingrid wears red—everybody else wears black soccer cleats. After a few minutes of stop-and-start conversation, the cab pulls up, and Ingrid races outside.

The next afternoon, Ingrid comes home from school, picks up the local newspaper in the driveway, leaves it on the kitchen table, and makes some hot chocolate. She glances at the front page—and nearly drops her mug.

LOCAL RESIDENT FOUND MURDERED, screams the headline. Katherine Eve Kovac was found murdered in her home. Anyone who spoke with her during the past few days is urged to talk with the police. That would include Ingrid.

Except that Ingrid doesn't think it's such a good idea for her to talk with the police. Even though that's exactly what her idol, Sherlock Holmes, would do. Then again, Sherlock Holmes never forgot to put on his red, very distinctive, soccer cleats and left them at the scene of the crime.

All of a sudden, life in Echo Falls has zoomed from dull to deadly.

Will Ingrid get her red soccer cleats back without being seen?

Will she get the lead in the play, beating out snippy Chloe, the most beautiful girl in school, who always gets whatever she wants?

Will she ever figure out how to calculate the amount of time it takes for two trucks traveling toward each other to meet?

Will she talk with Chief Strade, the chief of police—and the father of Joey, a boy she kind of likes?

And will she, Ingrid, follow in the footsteps of Sherlock Holmes, and solve the crime?

Find out, by reading *Down the Rabbit Hole: An Echo Falls Mystery*.

The Sudden Weirdness plotline is popular with younger teens. And no wonder: their own lives are being impacted by sudden, inexplicable changes in their brains, hearts, bodies, relationships, and roles in their world of home, neighborhood, and school. Like the characters in science fiction, mystery, and fantasy, teens have to improvise and learn on the job—the job of growing up.

Sudden Weirdness abounds in teen fiction. Janine wakes up from a coma, haunted by the spirit of her dead sister, Leonore—who wants to take over Janine's body for a second chance at life—in *Haunted Sister* (Littke 1998).

Maybe being the son of a human mother and the Greek god Poseiden is a better explanation for impetuosity than ADHD, as Percy discovers in *The Lightning Thief* (Riorden 2005). In *Whales on Stilts* (Anderson 2005), whales on stilts are coming to take over the world, and only Lily and her friends Katie and Jasper can stop them. Sent to Edgeview Alternative Middle School, Martin slowly realizes that his four new friends all possess paranormal hidden talents, which is the theme for *Hidden Talents* (Lubar 1999). In *Coraline* (Gaiman 2002), Coraline is trapped in another part of her house by a bizarre entity known as her Other Mother. Kidnapping a venomous performing spider changes Darren's life in *Cirque du Freak* (Shan 2001), the first volume of the *Saga of Darren Shan* series. In *Nightmare* (Nixon 2003), Emily thinks she recognizes some of the counselors at summer camp from the nightmare that has plagued her for years. Brothers Damien and Anthony have only seventeen days to spend the millions of English pound notes in the duffel bag that landed in Damien's hideout—in *Millions* (Boyce 2004). Meggie and her bookbinder father are kidnapped, and that is when Meggie discovers that her father has the ability to read a book so well that its characters come to life, in *Inkheart* (Funke 2003). Lina's job in *The City of Ember* (Du Prau 2003) is to be a messenger in an underground city whose lights are slowly dimming into darkness. Bobby wakes up one morning and discovers that he has become invisible in *Things Not Seen* (Clements 2002). Meg dies during a botched robbery, but gets a chance at redemption in *The Wish List* (Colfer 2000). Stricken by a brain tumor, Lucien falls asleep and wakes up in a parallel historical Venice in *Stravaganza: City of Masks* (Hoffman 2002). And Giannie becomes trapped inside a deadly virtual reality game in *Heir Apparent* (Vande Velde 2002).

Introduction and Program Outline

Once it is obvious that I will be talking about books, I introduce myself. I also like to quickly outline the program, which helps everybody to relax. Teens relax, because they know what to expect. I relax, because I have just reminded myself what I am going to do, rather than just plunging blindly ahead and hoping for the best. The outline also sets the style for seques between one section of the program and the next; that is, "I've talked about X. Now I'm going to talk about Y, and then I'll talk about Z." These seques knit the program together and keep all of us on track.

"Hi, I'm Kristine Mahood, I'm the teen librarian for Timberland Regional Library, and I spend my time working for you: visiting schools to talk about books, dreaming up teen library programs, writing booklists, and a lot more. I'd like to thank you and your teachers for giving class time so I could visit today. In between telling you about some good books, I'll show you the types of things you can get with a library card, I'll explain about library services and teen programs, and I'll end with a question . . . for you. The books I'll be talking about today are listed on the handout, so that if later today you think, 'what was that book about that guy who landed in a parallel life?' or 'what was that book about that girl whose family had to go into the Witness Protection Program?' you'll be able to find it on the handout. I've also included the library's teen Web site address, plus the library's street address, phone number, and the hours we're open. I've got plenty of handouts, plus booklists. Okay, how about a couple more booktalks, and then I'll talk about all of the things you can get with a library card."

Realistic Fiction Booktalks

After the Sudden Weirdness booktalks, I am ready to share a couple of books with more familiar settings. Realistic fiction addresses many of the issues that are going on in teen lives, such as expanding identity, new responsibilities at home, changing relationships with family, school challenges, new friends, and first love.

Double Dutch, by Sharon Draper

Everybody at school knows three things.

Delia is the smartest girl in 8th grade. She's good at math, and she's great at special projects, where a group of students brainstorms a topic, does the research, and writes up the results. Nobody brainstorms better than Delia. She's also a good friend, and the leader of the Queen Bees, the Double Dutch Jump Roping Team.

Randy is a fun guy. He's always there with a joke, a smile, and a helping hand. Randy is the kind of guy who doesn't have a care in the world. He's a good student, and the assistant manager of the Queen Bees.

Tabu and Titan Tolliver are Trouble with a capital T. They're big, they're mean, they dress in black, and they walk down the halls like they own the school, bumping people out of the way. And that special project they're working on for English? Everybody knows they're building a bomb or something.

Everybody at school knows all about Delia, Randy, and the Tolliver twins. But what *don't* they know?

They don't know that Delia takes notes in class in the teeniest handwriting in the world, so that if anybody sees it, all they see is a solid line. They don't know that when a book is assigned for English, Delia has to rent the video. They don't know that Delia doesn't know how to write ... because she doesn't know how to read. And so they don't know about the panic that grips Delia when she finds out that all students must pass the 8th grade competency exam, before they can continue to compete in sports.

They don't know that Randy's dad hasn't been home for two months. He's a long distance truck driver, and he's usually back home in several days.

Dad left Randy some money for food. But he didn't leave enough for rent, for electricity, or for paying the water bill.

They don't know that Tabu and Titan always wear black and always sit together because they don't know how else to act. They don't know what their lives were like before they came to their school.

Delia. Randy. Tabu and Titan. Everybody's going to find out a lot more about each other—and themselves—in a book that will make you wonder just how much you really know about people . . . who you *think* you know!

My Nights at the Improv, by Jan Siebold

I call it the 30-second delay.

You know what I'm talking about. Your 8th grade English teacher asks the class a question, waits, then calls on you: what do you think, Lizzie? Your brain goes blank. He moves on to someone else, and they come up with a good answer.

Thirty seconds later, you come up with a *brilliant* answer. Only you can't give it. 'Cause no one cares. The class has moved on.

This would be bad enough, but there's this girl in my class, Vanessa, who's been really nasty to me ever since Mom and I moved here, after Dad was killed in a car accident. Every time I say anything, Vanessa makes a little hissing sound, like a snake, just because on my first day I brought in a hot pink snakeskin purse. Of course, all her friends laugh. And then, she's the one who usually comes up with the good answer, after all I've done is mumble a big nothing.

So why am I telling you all this? Because I've been secretly watching this theater class that meets one night a week in the school auditorium. I'm sort of hiding up in the old projection booth, doing my homework, while Mom teaches an adult cooking class across the hall. Once class starts, I turn off the desk lamp so they can't see me up here. The class is about improvisation. Ben, the teacher, tells the students that there are no scripts in improv; instead, you have to come up with ideas on the spot. You have to dig into your head and come up with something fast, even though it might be not exactly perfect.

In other words, in improv, there's no 30-second delay.

In case I forgot to mention it, one of the students is Vanessa. And she's pretty good—of course.

Improv sure sounds like something I could use. Last week one of the exercises was alliteration, and the students had to make up sentences whose words all start with the same letter. Sounds weird, I know. But then it came up in my English class, and I actually did it, just like in improv, and it worked! So maybe this improve class can help me close up my 30-second delay, and—

Shhhh! Class is about to start. I'll turn out the desk lamp so they don't see me. I'll let you know later what Ben teaches them this time!

Not as Crazy as I Seem, by George Harrar

There's probably a few things that you like to do exactly the same way every time. Like eating an Oreo. Some people always pry off one chocolate wafer, eat it, scrape the icing off the other wafer with their teeth, and then eat the other wafer. Some people always wear their lucky socks every time they play basketball.

Fifteen-year-old Devon does a lot of things exactly the same way every time. Before walking in the front door of his new school, he waits until three people go in, so that he can be number four. Uh oh, missed it . . . so he has to wait for the next three people to go in, so that he can be number eight. He eats food in groups of four: four carrots, four sandwich halves, four cookies. Whenever something looks out of place, it really, *really* bothers him. For instance, there's a painting in a classroom that's hanging just a little bit crooked. Devon can hardly keep still in his chair, for wanting to jump up and straighten it.

Because of what happened seven years ago, Devon has put together an entire world of rituals and routines to keep all the chaos and disaster at a distance. Because of what happened seven years ago, Devon does things that get him asked to leave school. And his parents have to enroll him in another new school, which means they have to move.

So is this a depressing book about a teenage guy with obsessive compulsive disorder?

Well . . . it's pretty serious. But it's also pretty funny.

Devon is a smart guy, and he has a lot of funny stuff to say about things like eating dinner with parents, which can sometimes be an ordeal even if you don't have obsessive compulsive disorder. He's got funny things to say about the fact that he's not the only person who follows rituals and routines. After all, places like school couldn't run without some rituals and routines. And Devon's kind of happy, because for the first time in a long time, he's made a couple of friends. There's Tanya, a girl who eats lunch with him, and Ben, a purple-haired punk rocker. Devon really likes them both, but he has to wonder: if they knew what he was really like, would they still be his friends?

Sleeping Freshmen Never Lie, by David Lubar

Scott and his buddies are walking home from shooting hoops. Next day is the big day: the first day of high school.

"Any idea what it'll be like?" Scott asks. From what he's heard, being high school freshmen sounds like cattle walking up a ramp, clueless that they're headed for the slaughterhouse.

"Like a *Tomb Raider* movie," says Patrick. "Dangerous but cool."

"Same as middle school," groans Kyle. "Boring."

"No way! We'll be surrounded by gorgeous high school girls," drools Mitch.

"Like we have a chance with them," says Patrick.

"Girls *melt* when I get near them," brags Kyle.

"Mostly from the fumes," says Patrick.

Scott finds out that all the rumors about high school are true. Juniors and seniors bump into you in the halls, kick you when you're down, steal your lunch money, and date all the good-looking freshmen girls, who wouldn't be caught dead with freshmen guys. Classes are tough, the homework is staggering, and P.E. is like boot camp—for U.S. Special Forces.

But Scott decides he wants to do more than just exist in high school. He wants to excel. He wants to do something so that beautiful Julia, whom he's known since kindergarten, will give him a second look. She's written a column for the school newspaper? Scott joins the staff. Only to find out that Julia wrote just one "guest" column. Now Scott is stuck covering sports for a school whose teams lose all their games—and whose juniors and seniors don't like the way a lowly freshman reports on their losses. Julia's trying out for the school play? So does Scott. Julia doesn't get a part, and neither does Scott. But now he's tapped to be on the stage crew, and does all the work while the juniors and seniors sit around playing cards. Julia runs for student government? You can guess what happens.

In between the sore muscles from P.E., the brain strain from homework, and running for his life from angry football players, Scott starts finding out that high school isn't all bad. Old buddies drift away, but new friends show up. Wesley rescues him from juniors and seniors, and Lee, a girl with dyed green hair and tons of makeup and piercings, reads the same kind of books that Scott likes.

So maybe Patrick is turning out to be right about high school: dangerous, but actually kind of cool!

Realistic fiction reflects the growing complexity of younger teens' lives. Families and friends are changing. And school is more challenging, both in academic content and in social and moral dilemmas. Claire does not understand what makes the clique so important to Massie, in *The Clique* (Harrison 2004), and Maya does not understand why she was dropped from the clique, in *The Girls* (Koss 2000). Justin, bummed out by family troubles and best friend Ben's defection for a girlfriend, retreats into a mental blank he calls *The Big Nothing* (Fogelin 2004). In *Cheating Lessons* (Cappo 2002), high school brainiac Bernadette suspects that somebody cheated to advance her school in a classics competition. In *Stanford Wong Flunks Big-Time* (Yee 2005), when Stanford fails sixth grade English, has to take English in summer school so he does not flunk sixth grade. Worse, he is being tutored by the obnoxious know-it-all

Millicent Min, who first told the story of their summer, in *Millicent Min, Girl Genius* (Yee 2003). *First Crossing: Stories about Teen Immigrants* (Gallo 2004) features teens facing the twin challenges of crossing borders between childhood and teen years, and between other countries into the United States. Hank coaches next-door neighbor Tremont on coolness, Tremont tutors Hank in algebra, and they both cope with divorced parents in *Mixed-Up Doubles* (Eulo 2003). Twelve-year-old Sidney Mellon is sick of being tossed back and forth between his divorced parents—and bullied by his stepfather, his stepbrother, and kids at school in *Melonhead* (Guzman 2002).

What You Get with a Library Card

"So what can you get with a library card? Plenty!"

At this point in the program, I highlight the various library materials teens can check out with library cards: fiction and nonfiction books, magazines, books recorded on CD or audio cassette, CDs, DVDs, and videos. Holding up magazines, I talk about fashion, celebrities, humor, sports, skateboarding, science fiction, and other personal interests. Holding up a CD, I briefly list the many kinds of music available at the library, encouraging teens to expand their listening beyond the singers and bands with big advertising budgets. Holding up a DVD in one hand and a video in the other, I tell teens that the library's collection includes feature films new and classic, and how-to movies about everything real, such as pet care, jewelry making, and cool moves on bikes and skateboards.

Here is what I say while holding up a book recorded on CD in one hand and a book recorded on audio cassette in the other:

"So why would you listen to a book? Why wouldn't you just read one? Because sometimes, it's not so easy to read. You could be on the world's longest and most boring car trip, stuck in the back seat for hours. Reading makes you carsick. Instead, listen to a book on CD, or a book on tape. Or you could have to do something at home, like scrape the pizza off the ceiling of your room. It could take forever. Listen to a book on CD, or a book on tape. Or maybe you're strapped into the dentist's chair, or the orthodontist's chair. You could be there a long time. Listen to a book on CD, or a book on tape, and you'll have something else to think about besides what they're doing to your teeth."

I briefly explain how to reserve materials, which teens can do from any computer with an Internet connection, including computers at school. I also tell teens that with their library card, they have 24/7 access to our collection of research databases.

"It's Sunday night, that report is due tomorrow, and you need three more sources of information. If you can get to a computer with an Internet connection, visit Timberland Regional Library's Web site at www.trlib.org." I tell them that the address is listed on all of our handouts, booklists, and brochures. If I am in a classroom, I write the Web site address on the board. "Click on 'Research

Resources.' You'll see the same list of encyclopedias, magazine indexes, and more that are described in this brochure," I say, holding up the brochure that describes the library's databases. "Click on the resource you want, and it will ask you to type in your library card number. Type in your number, and then you can get what you need, whether it's some facts about a country, or a news photo, or maybe a picture of an animal. Be sure to pick up a copy of the research databases brochure, so you can see all the information you can get online."

"Since I've been talking a bit about real-life stuff, I guess I should share a few nonfiction books next, and then I'll tell you about some more fiction books."

Nonfiction Booktalks

By promoting nonfiction, you are showing teens the variety of materials they can get at the library. You are also expanding the definition of reading beyond fiction and school textbooks.

As children, younger teens turned to parents, other adults, and older siblings when they had questions. As teens, they still talk with parents and adults, but they also talk with one another, and they look for answers in teen magazines and on teen Web sites. Nonfiction books provide answers, too—and, like Web sites and magazines, they offer privacy. Nonfiction books offer answers about life information teens need to know, personal interests they want to explore, and school-related subjects.

Life Information

Books about physical development, care, grooming, nutrition, and fitness, like fashion and health magazines, can help younger teens answer the questions "What's happening to my body? How can I look good?" Self-help books about dealing with feelings and forming independent opinions will help teens answer the questions "How do I feel about this? What do I think?" Books about making the most out of middle school can help younger teens make the transition from elementary school. And just when they have figured out middle school, eighth graders realize that all too soon they will be hurled into high school. Classes will be harder, there will be more serious consequences for everything, and there is that "future" that parents and other adults are starting to talk about. Books about high school can assuage some of these anxieties.

Feeling Freakish? How to be Comfortable in Your Own Skin,
by Veronique le Jeune and Philippe Eliakim with Melissa Daly

Do you think your nose is too big? Are you too tall? Or maybe too short? Or maybe your friends have morphed into big strapping teenagers, and *nothing* is happening to you: you think you still look like a little kid. Maybe other teens at school laugh when you walk by, not because there's anything wrong with you, but because they are stuck-up brainless creeps.

Whatever the cause, sometimes being a teen means feeling like a freak. Your body is changing, sometimes slowly, and sometimes wham! overnight, so when you wake up and look in the mirror, you think, who *is* that? If you feel like a freak, then you need to read *Feeling Freakish? How to be Comfortable in Your Own Skin*. First, you'll find out that you're not alone: 75 percent of American teens can find at least one thing they don't like about the way they look. And next, there are ways to stop feeling like a freak. Forget the so-called hottie guys and girls you see in magazines: most of their photos are touched up to conceal *their* physical flaws. Be patient with your body: it's a work in progress, and it takes some time. Accept the fact that you're not perfect on the outside, and make the most of who you are on the inside. Find out things you're interested in, and go for it: sports, writing, music, art, whatever. Spend time with family and friends. Get comfortable in your own skin. Because everything changes . . . including your nose!

The number, variety, and formats of life-information nonfiction books for teens has increased dramatically in recent years. They lend themselves to booktalks and also to short shelf talks and quick show-and-tells—the more titles highlighted in a program, the better. In *Organizing from the Inside Out for Teens: The Foolproof System for Organizing Your Room, Your Time, and Your Life* (Morgenstern 2002), with newly complex lives, younger teens are ready for organizing. Bombarded by images of teen pop culture and social pressure from peers, younger teens also need to hear about *The Courage to be Yourself* (Desetta 2005). Teens talk about resisting being herded into group identities in *More Than a Label: Why What You Wear and Who You're with Doesn't Define Who You Are* (Muharrar 2002). *You Are Not Alone: Teens Talk about Life after the Loss of a Parent* (Hughes 2005) counsels teens experiencing this devastating loss.

Too Old for This, Too Young for That!: Your Survival Guide for the Middle School Years (Mosatche and Unger 2000) helps teens make the transition into the challenges and successes of middle school. Five middle school girls offer advice about life changes and challenges, in *Middle School: How to Deal* (Borden 2005). *The Middle School Survival Guide* (Erlbach 2003) offers another roadmap through middle school years. Boys in particular can benefit from hearing about *100 Things Guys Need to Know* (Zimmerman 2005). And when you read aloud "Don't Say These Things to Teachers" from pages 27 to 29 of *The Ultimate High School Survival Guide* (Dueber 1999), teens and teachers will roll in the aisles with laughter.

Personal Interests

Younger teens are also exploring their personal interests: boys, girls, fashion, music, computer game codes, celebrities, skateboarding, creating manga, movies, pet care, making things, and doing things. Teens are dealing with thoughts and feelings, and challenges and joys they never dreamed about when they were children. They are writing poetry, personal essays, short stories, and opinion pieces on social and other topics. Promoting teen writing, young adult librarians demonstrate that teens are contributing their knowledge about teen life to the world of books and reading.

Teen Knitting Club: Chill Out and Knit,
by Jennifer Wenger, Carol Abrams, and Maureen Lasher

It's happening all over the United States. In small towns, in big cities, at home, at school, in public libraries, in YMCAs, places of worship, and shops. It's happening among hip college students and 20-somethings, wise grannies, and laughing teen girls and guys. They do it for themselves, for each other, or to help other people.

What is it?

Knitting.

Wait a sec. Isn't knitting something that people did back in the olden days, before there were shopping malls and you had to make all your own clothes?

Yes. Knitting has been around for hundreds of years, because people either needed or wanted to make their own sweaters, hats, scarves, handbags, or other items. And it's still here, and bigger than ever, because knitting is also a way to express your creativity and your individuality. And because knitting is a great way to hang out with other people and to create things to give to people who need them.

Teen Knitting Club: Chill Out and Knit is your one-stop book for learning how to knit, how to make all kinds of projects, and how you can turn knitting into a reason to get together with friends and to contribute to your community. You'll find out about different kinds of yarns and needles (open book to show photo on page 16). You'll learn about stitches and knitting techniques (open book to show photo on page 46). Gorgeous color photos of clothes and other projects will inspire you (open book to show photos on pages 63, 83, 84, and 98). You might even get a knitting club together (open book to show photo on page 132). You can also connect with organizations that need such items as baby caps for newborns, warm shawls for people in the hospital, and afghans for people who need blankets.

And the comments of knitting girls and guys in this book will show you that knitting is for everybody!

"I like how people are brought together by knitting," says Coreen. "There's something special about this old pastime that people have been doing forever."

So start with a scarf or two, and you'll soon be making hats, sweaters, and more. It's all here, in *Teen Knitting: Chill Out and Knit.*

Craft, drawing, humor, and teen-writing books for teens help them express their creativity and explore their interests. *D.I.Y. Girl: The Real Girl's Guide to Making Everything from Lip Gloss to Lamps* (Bonnell 2003) is a fast, fun guide to creating gifts, beauty products, clothing, and room décor. *Button Girl: More than 20 Cute-as-a-Button Projects* (Bruder 2005) elevates the humble button to art. Girls can also learn how to make their own lotions, rinses, and other grooming and beauty products in *Beauty Trix for Cool Chix* (Naylor 2003). Teens can learn how to have fun with their rooms in *Have Fun with Your Room: 28 Cool Projects for Teens* (Jennings 2001). Using materials as diverse as beads, feathers, and wingnuts from Mom and Dad's toolbox, teens can learn making jewelry, from *Jewelry Making: Basic Techniques* (Moody 1998). Teens who watch anime and read manga might be intrigued by such books as *How to Draw Action Dragon Ball Z* (Watson 2002) and *Draw Your Own Manga: All the Basics* (Nagatomo 2003). *So, You Wanna Be a Comic Book Artist?* (Amara and Mhan 2001) includes interviews with kids and teens who are creating and publishing comics. Mechanically minded teens looking for science fair projects can find them in *How to Build Your Own Prize-Winning Robot* (Sobey 2002). Comic strip feline supreme Garfield explains it all in *Garfield's Guide to Everything* (Davis 2004). Teens tell their own stories in their own words in such books as Canfield's *Chicken Soup for the Teenage Soul* series.

School-Related Subjects

School media specialists and teachers may suggest that you booktalk a few titles that will pique teens' interest in school-related topics. This is your opportunity to booktalk such books as biographies of people overcoming adversity, histories of past or current events, or art books. Teens are intrigued by extreme real-life situations such as natural or man-made disasters, and wonder how they would react to them. Younger teens also enjoy illustrated books about such science-related topics as bugs, dinosaurs, machines, UFOs, and other freaky true (or untrue) subjects.

An American Plague: The True and Terrifying Story of the Yellow Fever Epidemic of 1793, by Jim Murphy

In the summer of 1793, with the American Revolution over and the new government in place, nobody in Philadelphia, Pennsylvania, was much inclined to worry if a few people got sick from fever. After all, fevers came every hot summer, and they went away in the fall. And besides, everybody was just too busy! People were building up businesses, going to school, going to the market, unloading ships at the docks, hanging out in coffeehouses, and having a good time. Nobody worried about the fact that eight people died in two houses on one street, in just one week in early August. Fever? Yes, well, that's normal.

But this was no ordinary summer fever.

It killed.

On one day, 12 people died. On the next, 13 people. Like a poisonous yellow fog the fever crept into every block, every street, and every house. More people got sick. Church bells tolled nonstop as dozens of people died, then hundreds. As many as 20,000 people raced out of the city, out of a total population of 50,000. Shops closed. Schools closed. People shut themselves up in their houses so they wouldn't catch the fever. Fewer employees showed up for work, so city services slowed down to almost nothing. Families broke apart, as some died, others lay sick in their beds, and others deserted them. Doctors tried one remedy, then another. And there were people who stayed to help, to take care of the sick and to keep Philadelphia from turning into a ghost town. This is the true story of the epidemic that half-destroyed a city, and of the heroic men and women who fought to save their fellow citizens.

Historical figures become people and contemporary celebrities tell their stories, in biographies and memoirs. *Frederick Douglass: For the Great Family of Man* (Burchard 2003) chronicles the life of the abolitionist and thinker. *The Diary of a Young Girl: The Definitive Edition* (Frank 1995) introduces younger teens to Anne Frank, a teenager who speaks across the decades. Tony Hawk describes how he dreamed up and tried out extraordinary skateboard moves, and succeeded in raising the profile of the sport, in *Tony Hawk: Professional Skateboarder* (Hawk and Mortimer 2002). And thirteen-year-old Samantha Abeel tells her story in *My Thirteenth Winter: A Memoir* (Abeel 2003), during which her mathematics learning disability was finally diagnosed, and her life improved.

Well-written history offers both facts and perspective. *Fighting for Honor: Japanese Americans and World War II* (Cooper 2000) chronicles both the heroic service of Japanese-Americans soldiers during World War II and the imprisonment of civilians in internment camps. Teens who are intrigued by survival and rescue stories will enjoy hearing about *Blizzard: The Storm That Changed America* (Murphy 2000), the story of the snowstorm that shut down the Northeast in the spring of 1888. Teens intrigued by speed and true adventure will be thrilled to read *The Mail Must Go Through: The Story of the Pony Express* (Rau 2005). Teens take voting for granted, but the women of the United States had to fight long and hard for this right, as retold in *With Courage and Cloth: Winning the Fight for a Woman's Right to Vote* (Bausum 2004).

Heart and Soul Booktalks

By this point in the program, teens are accustomed to the booktalk format. Their curiosity was piqued by the sudden weirdness books; they have been mulling over realistic fiction and nonfiction, and now they are ready to connect with books that carry more emotional resonance. The stories are more complex, the characters are more thoughtful and emotionally accessible, the settings are more detailed, and the language of the booktalks flows, eddies, and flows again. Moving from one booktalk into the next, we are all in the zone. I booktalk a mix of realistic fiction, fantasy, science fiction, historical fiction, maybe a serial comic romance, a suspense-darkened mystery, or high-stakes action novel. I might read a poem from one book, or tell a story from a short story collection.

For sixth grade audiences, I booktalk a mix of older children's books and younger teens' books, because younger teens are not that far away from childhood interests. For seventh and eighth grade audiences, I booktalk a mix of younger and older teens' books, because younger teens are looking forward to being older teens. Many books featuring older teen characters are just as accessible and age-appropriate in content and writing style as books featuring younger teen characters. Younger teens can connect with these books on an emotional level—through humor or heartache—without being buffeted by the swearing, implied or explicit sexual activity, or protracted violence that appears in some books written for much older teens. I like to conclude this section with a book that packs an emotional wallop.

Takedown, by Joyce Sweeney

The amazing thing was, no one screamed.

Joe, his sister Elizabeth, and their friends ordered pizza for their Friday night party, watching a big wrestling match on TV. Mom left for her writing class. She didn't feel right about leaving the house. Not because she hadn't done the assignment or anything, but because of the news on TV: Quentin Dorn, a college student, had shot three people and was still at large. Don't open the door, Mom told Joe.

When the doorbell rang, Joe answered it. The delivery guy brought in the pizzas—and a gun. Joe recognized him immediately.

No one screamed.

No one could believe it.

"Is there anybody else in the house?" Quentin Dorn yelled.

"No, just us," Joe answered.

"Where's the car, in the garage?"

"Mom took it, she won't be back 'til 10 o'clock."

Now Dorn really gets angry. He'd taken the pizza delivery guy's uniform so he could get into the house and steal the car and escape, but there was no car!

The phone rings. It's the F.B.I. And so begins the long night, as Dorn gets more and more angry and out of control, and Joe, Elizabeth, and their friends have to put their fear aside and come up with a plan to save their lives.

Flipped, by Wendelin Van Draanen

For six years, Bryce has been avoiding Juli. It started back in second grade, when his family moved into the neighborhood. There they were, on a bright, sunny day, unloading the moving van and minding their own business. Suddenly this blonde cannonball shot into the moving van. Her name was Juli. She'd spotted Bryce, and now she was looking for him. Mom thought Juli was cute. Dad thought she was loud. Lynette, Bryce's older sister, thought she was ridiculous. Bryce thought she was scary, and way too obnoxious and pushy. And so for six years, all the way up to eighth grade, Bryce has been avoiding Juli.

For six years, all the way up to eighth grade, Juli has been chasing Bryce. Because the moment she'd seen him on that sunny moving day, her heart had flipped over. His blue eyes. His smile. The way he walked. The way he talked. Everything. Juli has been doing her best to get Bryce to notice her. For six years she's smiled at him, she's sat next to him in class, she's even given him eggs from the chickens she's raised. But nothing's worked.

And so in eighth grade, Juli gives up. She accepts reality. Bryce is a selfish, stuck-up snob.

One day, Bryce looks over at Juli. For once, she doesn't look back. But . . . how could he have not noticed? She's wonderful! And Bryce's heart flips over.

Now what?

Hush, by Jacqueline Woodson

Hush. Don't say anything. If you say anything about where you used to live, your old friends, your old school, even your old name, they could find you.

Evie can't talk about where she used to live, in Colorado. She can't talk about her best friend forever, Lulu. She can't even tell people her real name, Toswiah.

One night Dad saw two fellow policemen shoot an African American teenager. They said they thought he was going to pull a gun on them. He had no gun, and he died. Dad had always been best friends with the other cops in his precinct. It didn't matter to them that they were white and Dad was African American. They were all cops, and they all stood together. In fact, the other cops had been sort of like uncles to Toswiah—sorry, Evie—and her older sister, Cameron—no, wait, Anna. But when Dad decided to testify at the trial, the threats began, and all that one-big-happy-family stuff went out the window.

Hush. Don't say anything.

After the trial, the family was put into the Witness Protection Program, told to change their names, and moved far away. And one by one, each member of the family moves away again—from one another. Mom moves into her new church. Dad moves into depression. Anna moves into anger.

But Evie doesn't want to move away from her family. She knows she has no place to go but where she is. Trouble is, she hates it. She hates what's happened to her family. Mom spends all of her time at church. Dad is slipping away, day by day, past sadness and depression and into mental illness. Anna is so angry that Evie can't talk to her.

Torn from the past, not accepting the present, and not seeing any real future . . . Someone's got to break through the hush that has silenced the family. Could that someone be Evie?

Waiting for Sarah, by Bruce McBay and James Heneghan

It happened so fast.

One minute, Mike and his little sister were in the back seat, Mom was talking, and Dad was driving. They're on their way to their usual end-of-summer week at the cabin. Mike's thinking about junior year in high school.

The next minute, Mike wakes up in the hospital and finds out that a drunken driver smashed into the car, killing Mom, Dad, and his sister, and crushing Mike's legs so badly that they both had to be amputated below the knee.

Stunned by grief, Mike is angry and bitter, cursing at nurses, doctors, and his friends. After months in rehab, Mike is brought home, to his new home, with his Aunt Norma. He refuses to even think about going back to school. "What's the point?" he asks Aunt Norma, and Robbie, the only friend who's stuck by him the whole time. What's the point of school, of graduating, of anything? His life is over.

But one day Aunt Norma insists: Mike is going back to school. It's been a year since the accident, and it's time to go back.

"No way," says Mike. "I'm not repeating junior year while everybody else is a senior."

"You don't have to," says Aunt Norma, and she explains how Mike can go back as an incoming senior and make up junior year with a few projects. One project is to write a history of the high school.

"Oh, that oughta be a best seller!" Mike says.

But he takes the deal. Mike rolls into his first day of senior year. People crowd around him. We're so sorry, we're so sorry, they all say. And Mike knows they mean well. But he notices that everybody looks him straight in the eyes—and only in the eyes. Nobody looks where his lower legs used to be.

So he starts the "special project," the school history. All the records of the school—yearbooks, school newspapers—are in a storage room in the school library. The place is a mess. It's dark, it's dusty, and although Mike hates to admit it, when the editor of the school newspaper says she'll send a younger student over to help him out, he's relieved. At least there'll be somebody to get the stuff down from the top shelves.

So Mike is working away one day, and feels a cool little breeze. Somebody's in the doorway. He wheels around. A girl stares at him. She's short, skinny, and has got curly hair. She squints.

"What happened to your *legs*?" she asks.

Who is *this* twerp? Mike thinks. Then it hits him. She must be the kid that the editor sent over. Some freshman.

Her name is Sarah. She asks him a million questions. She laughs. She hums. She jokes around. She drives Mike nuts. And she makes him laugh. She makes him care. And so every day, Mike finds himself waiting for Sarah. Until the day that he finds out that just as Sarah has helped him, now it's his turn to help Sarah.

While books in the heart and soul section come from many genres—realistic fiction, fantasy, historical fiction, science fiction, romance, and others—their intent is to make and keep an emotional connection with younger teens. The sudden weirdness booktalks got their attention, and appealed to their curiosity and intellect. Heart and soul books appeal to their emotions. Sometimes the emotions are light, and sometimes they are heavy. Resourceful apprentice shoemaker Phoenix braves evil spells, wicked princesses, and her own self-doubts to solve the mystery of why the twelve princesses dance their shoes to shreds each night, in *The Phoenix Dance* (Calhoun 2005). Twelve-year-old Matthew looks up to his older brother, Kevin, and wonders why other teens ridicule, harass, and threaten him, in *The Rainbow Kite* (Shyer 2002). In *Perfect* (Friend 2004), thirteen-year-old Isabelle retreats into bulimia so she can be perfect, and forgets that Dad is dead. *Soldier Boys* (Hughes 2001) tells parallel stories of two teens—Dieter, fifteen and Spencer, seventeen—who go through training in the German and American armies and meet on the battlefield. In *Double Identity* (Haddix 2005), Bethany does not understand why Mom and Dad have dumped her with Aunt Myrlie, until she slowly unravels the skein of secrets wound around her birth. In *Heck Superhero* (Leavitt 2004), Heck is locked out of the apartment when Mom does not pay the rent, and now she has disappeared and he has got to do enough Good Deeds to score a few dollars so he can eat. *Mable Riley: A Record of Humdrum, Peril, and Romance* (Jocelyn 2004) is Mable's 1901 diary, recounting her new life in rural Ontario province as the assistant to the new teacher, her older sister Viola. Matt is fourteen, in trouble, and exiled to a village in the English countryside, where he discovers a witch-driven plot to open the raven's gate, in *Raven's Gate* (Horowitz 2005). *Money Hungry* (Flake 2001) tells the story of Raspberry Hill, who is money hungry and sells candy and cleans houses so she and Momma will not ever have to live on the streets again. Koji could not cut it as a dye maker, and resists new training as a ninja until war devastates his home in *Blue Fingers: A*

Ninja's Tale (Whitesel 2004). Brenda finds a library card where her beloved TV used to sit and takes it to the public library, where she finds a book about her life up to page 15, when she first turned on the TV, one of the short stories in *The Library Card* (Spinelli 1997). Jim is the shortest player on his middle school basketball team and learns about perseverance and courage in the face of tragedy from Nana, his grandmother, in *House of Sports* (Russo 2002). In *Rodzina* (Cushman 2003), Rodzina and the other kids and teens on the Orphan Train in 1881 know that they are being shipped West not to be "adopted," but to be sold as slaves to farmers. The police say fifteen-year-old Luke can stay out of juvenile hall if he works as a guide runner with Jodi, a girl who is blind, in *On the Run* (Coleman 2004). Hannah lives at the edge of the forest as a folk healer, brewing medicines for the villagers and pondering her origins, in *Treasure at the Heart of the Tanglewood* (Pierce 2001).

Upcoming Teen Events

After the concluding booktalk in the heart and soul section, we all need a little emotional respite. And so, before delivering my final booktalk, I lighten the mood with a bit of news about upcoming teen events. Holding up the relevant poster or events brochure, I highlight craft workshops, focus groups, cafes, book discussion groups, and so on. I speak in a quiet, conversational tone, because I can tell, by looking around the room, that younger teens are still absorbing the booktalks. After reminding them to pick up a copy of the events brochure, I tell them that I have just one more book to share, and then I have a question for them.

Always Leave Them Laughing

I like to end the program by booktalking a funny book, or a romantic comedy. I start out talking in a regular, reasonable voice, then pick up inflection and speed until we are all racing pell mell for the fun finish.

Dork in Disguise, by Carol Gorman

First day of school. New town, new school, and Jerry is standing off to one side, squinting, waiting for the right moment to walk in. It's got to be just the right moment, because this year is going to be different.

This year, Jerry is *not* going to be a dork.

Jerry spent the summer studying teen magazines, trying out hair gel, practicing cool lines, and resisting the urge to build science fair projects. And now all that hard work is going to pay off, because Jerry has just spotted the most beautiful girl, and he knows that if he can just—

"Why don't you put on your glasses?"

Jerry turns to see a girl looking straight at him.

"Huh? What glasses?"

"The glasses you were wearing this morning."

"How did you know?"

"You're squinting," the girl explained. "Plus, you have little dents on the side of your nose. You took your glasses off less than an hour ago. Trying to change your image?"

Jerry was astounded. Could this girl read his mind?

No, but she's smart. Her name is Brenda, she wears glasses, she's great at science, and she offers to give Jerry tips on being cool. She helps him to rip his jeans. She coaches him on the art of a super-confident, show-off walk. She even gives him advice on how to start a conversation with Cinnamon, that beautiful girl.

And all of Brenda's advice works! Jerry is cool, he's accepted by the popular kids, and Cinnamon is smiling at him. But if everything's so great, how come what Jerry really wants is to hang out with Brenda and...no, no, NO...join the science club?

Funny Girl Book Booktalk

Both juvenile and young adult novels abound with humor, much of it exploding in school settings. Twins Meg and Edward take turns sarcastically narrating chapters in *Never Mind* (Avi and Vail, 2004). Cody is flunking out of high school, until he transfers to a magnet school for a very special kind of student, in *Vampire High* (Rees 2002). *Lily's Ghosts* (Ruby 2003) are a big drag for Lily, who is particularly plagued by a spiteful teen beauty queen who died before the pageant. Although it also explores Moose's relationship with his sister Natalie, who suffers from autism, a title like *Al Capone Does My Shirts* (Choldenko 2004) offers great punch-line potential. Fourteen-year-old Jamie tells the roller-coaster ride story in *How My Private, Personal Journal Became a Bestseller* (DeVillers 2004). Gary Paulsen (2003) recounts the insanely stupid stunts he and his friends used to pull, in *How Angel Peterson Got His Name: And Other Outrageous Tales of Extreme Sports*. Noah and Abbey vow to stand by their dad, in jail for attempting to sink a riverboat that was dumping sewage into the waters off the Florida Keys, in *Flush* (Hiaasen 2005). Tenth grader Justine is amazed to discover that she is falling for a younger guy—Mike, her eighth-grade best friend—in *Lombardo's Law* (Wittlinger 1993). Eighth grader Calman leaves Boston for a two-week visit with raucous pen pal Rizzy in Walla Walla, Washington, who turns out to be a girl, in *Palms to the Ground* (Stolls 2005).

Let's All Talk about Books

Now comes the really fun part of the program. Grab some paper, a pen, and a surface to write on, like a picture-book format nonfiction book.

"I've told you about some good books, now I need you to tell me about good books. What do you recommend? What do you think people should read? I need to hear from as many people as possible, because I'm always looking for good books to add to the library and I need your help."

Smile. Create an open mood. Be friendly and encouraging. Hold your pen at the ready, which tells teens that what they have to say is important enough for you to write it down. Teens are accustomed to writing down what adults have to say. Now an adult is going to write down what *they* have to say.

Sometimes teens may not respond immediately. Try tossing out one of the titles you just booktalked.

"So did you like the sound of *Vampire High?* Or *Double Identity*? Remind you of other books you like? And hey, you can also mention books you *don't* like. Because by talking about books you don't like, we can figure out the opposite: books you might like."

All it takes to get the bonfire started is for one teen to mention one book.

"I really like the *Pendragon* series," says a boy.

Fan that flame. If you have read one of the books about fourteen-year-old Bobby Pendragon's adventures in time and space, say so, and mention one quick thing about it. Then ask a few follow-up questions so that the teen can expand on what he liked about the book.

"What was that book about? What was so good about it? What did you like about it?"

If you can think of a similar book that the teen might like, mention it. Avoid prosing on and on: remember, this section of the program is not about you, it is about teens and what they like to read.

While it is good to get a conversation going, avoid focusing on any one teen too long. Keep making it clear that you want to hear from as many teens as possible, so look or walk around the room, and keep asking for titles. After that first teen, another will feel emboldened to speak up, and then another, and pretty soon the titles are flying as thick and fast as sparks from a fire, and you are scribbling them down.

"This is great, this is so great! Thank you! And if you think of other books that you like, and that you think other teens might like, please let me know! Talk to me after the program, phone me up at the library, or stop by the desk at the library. I want to know what you like to read, so the library can get more of those books. And thank you again: you've been a great audience. See you at the library!"

A lot is going on in this concluding section of the program, which can last from five to ten minutes.

First, you are encouraging teens to talk about books. You are changing the focus of the program from what you recommend to what teens recommend—to fellow teens.

Second, you are gathering input for collection development. There is no better way to find out what teens like to read than to ask them. It is true that some teens may not speak up because they are shy, or because they are reading books that they do not think are popular, or because they do not read very much and have little to say. That is why it is important to emphasize that teens can talk to you at any time about what they like to read, not just in this public forum. Teachers and school media specialists are also keen to know what types of books appeal to 'tweens and younger teens so that they can keep recommending books through readers' advisory, displays, booklists, and other methods.

Third, you are performing—and promoting—readers' advisory service. You are demonstrating to teens that you can tell them about many more books beyond the list of books you just booktalked, and that by extension the public library is a great source for more good books. All the better when teachers or school media specialists chime in with recommendations, demonstrating the readers' advisory services they offer to 'tweens and teens.

And fourth, once again, you are encouraging teens to talk about books. Teens who read often hear about good books from their friends, or other teens, and they are always looking for more to read. Teens who do not read very much also have a chance to hear about good books from other teens. By opening up the program for book recommendations, you are creating the conditions for peer-to-peer marketing.

CONCLUSION

When you return to your library, create a poster reading, "What were those books the librarian talked about at school?" and assemble a display of the books you just booktalked, plus copies of your handout. Give a copy of your handout to library staff so that they can help teens who come in looking for the books. Type up a list of the books that teens recommended, and send a copy to the school media specialist. You might also send your youth materials selector a list of books that teens recommended. Think of their suggestions as a local best seller list.

Booktalking in public and private schools is a great way to connect younger teens with reading and books. Consider taking your show to other venues. Parent groups, homeschool groups, literacy groups, local business associations, and other organizations are often looking for guest speakers. Many parents and other adults know what the public library offers for children, but may not be as aware of the books, other collections, resources, services, programs, and volunteer opportunities that libraries offer to teens. With concerns over adolescent literacy on the rise, and a dazzling array of books to promote, there has never been a better time to booktalk to teens.

REFERENCES AND SUGGESTED READINGS

Abeel, Samantha. *My Thirteenth Winter: A Memoir*. New York: Orchard Books, 2003.

Abrahams, Peter. *Down the Rabbit Hole: An Echo Falls Mystery.* New York: HarperCollins, 2005.

Amara, Philip, and Pop Mhan. *So, You Wanna Be a Comic Book Artist? How to Create Your Own Superheroes, Sell Your Strip, and Become Famous!* Hillsboro, OR: Beyond Words Publishing, 2001.

Anderson, M. T. *Whales on Stilts.* Orlando, FL: Harcourt, 2005.

Anderson, Sheila B., and Kristine Mahood. "The Inner Game of Booktalking." *Voice of Youth Advocates* 24, no. 2 (2001): 107–110.

Avi and Rachel Vail. *Never Mind.* New York: HarperCollins, 2004.

Bausum, Ann. *With Courage and Cloth: Winning the Fight for a Woman's Right to Vote.* Washington, DC: National Geographic, 2004.

Biancarosa, Gina, and Catherine E. Snow. *Reading Next—A Vision for Action and Research in Middle and High School Literacy: A Report to Carnegie Corporation of New York.* Washington, DC: Alliance for Excellent Education, 2004.

Bonnell, Jennifer. *D.I.Y. Girl: The Real Girl's Guide to Making Everything from Lip Gloss to Lamps.* New York: Puffin Books, 2003.

Borden, Sara. *Middle School: How to Deal.* San Francisco: Chronicle Books, 2005.

Boyce, Frank Cottrell. *Millions.* New York: HarperCollins, 2004.

Bruder, Mikyla. *Button Girl: More than 20 Cute-as-a-Button Projects.* San Francisco: Chronicle Books, 2005.

Burchard, Peter. *Frederick Douglass: For the Great Family of Man.* New York: Atheneum Books for Young Readers, 2003.

Calhoun, Dia. *The Phoenix Dance.* New York: Farrar, Straus and Giroux, 2005.

Canfield, Jack. *Chicken Soup for the Teenage Soul.* Deerfield Beach, FL: Health Communications, 1997.

Cappo, Nan Willard. *Cheating Lessons.* New York: Atheneum, 2002.

Chall, Jeanne. *Stages of Reading Development.* New York: McGraw-Hill, 1983.Choldenko, Gennifer. *Al Capone Does My Shirts.* New York: G.P. Putnam, 2004.

Clements, Andrew. *Things Not Seen.* New York: Philomel Books, 2002.

Clinton, Patrick. "The Crisis You Don't Know about, Part One." *Book* (September/October 2002): L4–L9.

Coleman, Michael. *On the Run.* New York: Dutton Children's Books, 2004.

Colfer, Eoin. *The Wish List*. New York: Miramax Books/Hyperion Books for Children, 2000.

Cooper, Michael L. *Fighting for Honor: Japanese Americans and World War II*. New York: Clarion Books, 2000.

Cushman, Karen. *Rodzina*. New York: Clarion Books, 2003.

Davis, Jim. *Garfield's Guide to Everything*. New York: Ballantine Books, 2004.

Desetta, Al, ed. *The Courage to Be Yourself: True Stories by Teens about Cliques, Conflicts, and Overcoming Peer Pressure*. Minneapolis, MN: Free Spirit Publishing, 2005.

DeVillers, Julia. *How My Private, Personal Journal Became a Bestseller*. New York: Dutton Children's Books, 2004.

Donelson, Kenneth L., and Alleen Pace Nilsen. *Literature for Today's Young Adults*. New York: Longman, 1997.

Draper, Sharon. *Double Dutch*. New York: Atheneum Books, 2002.

Dueber, Julianne. *The Ultimate High School Survival Guide*. Princeton, NJ: Peterson, 1999.

Du Prau, Jeanne. *The City of Ember*. New York: Random House, 2003.

Erlbach, Arlene. *The Middle School Survival Guide: How to Survive from the Day Elementary School Ends Until the Second High School Begins*. New York: Books for Young Readers, 2003.

Eulo, Elena Yates. *Mixed-Up Doubles*. New York: Holiday House, 2003.

Flake, Sharon G. *Money Hungry*. New York: Hyperion, 2001.

Fogelin, Adrian. *The Big Nothing*. Atlanta, GA: Peachtree Publishers, 2004.

Frank, Anne. *The Diary of a Young Girl: The Definitive Edition*. New York: Bantam Books, 1995.

Friend, Natasha. *Perfect*. Minneapolis, MN: Milkweek Editions, 2004.

Funke, Cornelia. *Inkheart*. Translated from the German by Anthea Bell. New York: Chicken House, 2003.

Gaiman, Neil. *Coraline*. New York: HarperCollins, 2002.

Gallo, Donald, ed. *First Crossing: Stories about Teen Immigrants*. Cambridge, MA: Candlewick, 2004.

Gaskins, Pearl Fuyo. *I Believe in . . ..: Christian, Jewish, and Muslim Young People Speak about Their Faith*. Chicago: Cricket Books, 2005.

Gorman, Carol. *Dork in Disguise*. New York: HarperCollins, 1999.

Guzman, Michael de. *Melonhead*. New York: Farrar, Straus and Giroux, 2002.

Haddix, Margaret Peterson. *Double Identity*. New York: Simon & Schuster Children's Publishing, 2005.

Harrar, George. *Not as Crazy as I Seem*. Boston: Houghton Mifflin, 2003.

Harrison, Lisi. *The Clique*. New York: Little, Brown, 2004.

Hawk, Tony, and Sean Mortimer. *Tony Hawk: Professional Skateboarder*. New York: Regan Books, 2002.

Herald, Diana Tixier. *Teen Genreflecting: A Guide to Reading Interests*. Westport, CT: Libraries Unlimited, 2003.

Hiaasen, Carl. *Flush*. New York: Alfred A. Knopf, 2005.

Hoffman, Mary. *Stravaganza: City of Masks*. New York: Bloomsbury, 2002.

Horowitz, Anthony. *Raven's Gate*. New York: Scholastic Press, 2005.

Hughes, Dean. *Soldier Boys*. New York: Atheneum, 2001.

Hughes, Lynne. *You Are Not Alone: Teens Talk about Life after the Loss of a Parent*. New York: Scholastic, 2005.

Jennings, Lynette. *Have Fun with Your Room: 28 Cool Projects for Teens*. New York: Simon Pulse, 2001.

Jocelyn, Marthe. *Mable Riley: A Reliable Record of Humdrum, Peril, and Romance*. Cambridge, MA: Candlewick, 2004.

Jones, Jami. "Priority Male." *School Library Journal* 51, no. 3 (2005): 37.

Koss, Amy Goldman. *The Girls*. New York: Dial Books for Young Readers, 2000.

Lawrence, Michael. *A Crack in the Line*. New York: Greenwillow Books, 2004.

Leavitt, Martine. *Heck Superhero*. Asheville, NC: Front Street, 2004.

Le Juene, Veronique, and Phillippe Eliakim, with Melissay Daly. *Feeling Freakish? How to Be Comfortable in Your Own Skin*. New York: Sunscreen, 2004.

Littke, Lael. *Haunted Sister*. New York: Henry Holt, 1998.

Lubar, David. *Hidden Talents*. New York: Tom Doherty Associates, 1999.

————. *Sleeping Freshmen Never Lie*. New York: Dutton Books, 2005.

MacHale, D. J. *Pendragon: An Adventure through Time and Space*. New York: Simon & Schuster Books for Young Readers, 2002.

Manzo, Kathleen Kennedy. "Reading Researchers Outline Elements Needed to Achieve Adolescent Literacy." *Education Week* 24, no. 8 (2004): 10.

McBay, Bruce, and James Heneghan. *Waiting for Sarah*. Custer, WA: Orca, 2003.

Mood, Jo. *Jewelry Making: Basic Techniques*. New York: Foster Publishing, 1998.

Moore, David W., Thomas W. Bean, Deanna Birdyshaw, and James Rycik. "Adolescent Literacy: A Position Statement." *Journal of Adolescent and Adult Literacy* 43, no. 1 (September 1999): 97–112.

Morgenstern, Julie, with Jessi Morgenstern-Colon. *Organizing from the Inside Out for Teens: The Foolproof System for Organizing Your Room, Your Time, and Your Life*. New York: Henry Holt, 2002.

Mosatche, Harriet S., and Karen Unger. *Too Old for This, Too Young for That!: Your Survival Guide for the Middle-School Years*. Minneapolis, MN: Free Spirit Publishing, 2000.

Muharrar, Aisha. *More Than a Label: Why What You Wear and Who You're with Doesn't Define Who You Are*. Minneapolis, MN: Free Spirit Press, 2002.

Murphy, Jim. *An American Plague: The True and Terrifying Story of the Yellow Fever Epidemic of 1793*. New York: Clarion Books, 2003.

————. *Blizzard!: The Storm That Changed America*. New York: Scholastic Press, 2000.

Nagatomo, Haruno. *Draw Your Own Manga: All the Basics*. Tokyo, Japan: Coade and Kodansha International, 2003.

Naylor, Caroline. *Beauty Trix for Cool Chix*. New York: Watson-Guptill, 2003.

Nixon, Joan Lowery. *Nightmare*. New York: Delacorte Press, 2003.

Paulsen, Gary. *How Angel Peterson Got His Name: And Other Outrageous Tales of Extreme Sports*. New York: Wendy Lamb Books, 2003.

Pearl, Nancy. *Now Read This II: A Guide to Mainstream Fiction*. Greenwood Village, CO: Libraries Unlimited, 2002.

Pierce, Meredith Ann. *Treasure at the Heart of the Tanglewood*. New York: Viking, 2001.

Rau, Margaret. *The Mail Must Go Through: The Story of the Pony Express*. Greensboro, NC: Morgan Reynolds, 2005.

Rees, Douglas. *Vampire High*. New York: Delacorte Press, 2002.

Riorden, Rick. *The Lightning Thief*. New York: Hyperion Books, 2005.

Ruby, Laura. *Lily's Ghosts*. New York: HarperCollins, 2003.

Russo, Marisabina. *House of Sports*. New York: Greenwillow Books, 2002.

Saricks, Joyce. *Readers' Advisory Service in the Public Library*. Chicago: American Library Association, 2005.

Scrimger, Richard. *The Nose from Jupiter*. Toronto, ON: Tundra Books, 1998.

Shan, Darren. *Cirque Du Freak #1: A Living Nightmare*. New York: Little, Brown, 2001.

Shusterman, Neal. *Full Tilt*. New York: Simon & Schuster Books for Young Readers, 2003.

Shyer, Marlene Fanta. *The Rainbow Kite*. New York: Marshall Cavendish, 2002.

Siebold, Jan. *My Nights at the Improv*. Morton Grove, IL: Albert Whitman, 2005.

Sobey, Edwin J. C. *How to Build Your Own Prize-Winning Robot*. Berkeley Heights, NJ: Enslow Publishers, 2002.

Spinelli, Jerry. *The Library Card*. New York: Scholastic, 1997.

Stolls, Amy. *Palms to the Ground*. New York: Farrar, Straus and Giroux, 2005.

Strauch, Barbara. *The Primal Teen: What the New Discoveries about the Teenage Brain Tell Us about Our Kids*. New York: Doubleday, 2003.

Sweeney, Joyce. *Takedown*. New York: Marshall Canvendish, 2004.

Van Draanen, Wendelin. *Flipped*. New York: Alfred A. Knopf, 2002.

Vande Velde, Vivian. *Heir Apparent*. San Diego, CA: Harcourt, 2002.

Walker, Sally M. *Fossil Fish Found Alive: Discovering the Coelacanth*. Minneapolis, MN: Carolrhoda Books, 2002.

Watson, B. S. *How to Draw Action Dragonball Z*. New York: Scholastic, 2002.

Wenger, Jennifer, Carol Abrams, and Maureen Lasher. *Teen Knitting Club: Chill Out and Knit.* New York: Artisan, 2004.

Whitesel, Cheryl. *Blue Fingers: A Ninja's Tale.* New York: Clarion Books, 2004.

Wittlinger, Ellen. *Lombardo's Law.* Boston: Houghton Mifflin, 1993.

Woodson, Jacqueline. *Hush.* New York: G.P. Putnam, 2002.

Yee, Lisa. *Millicent Min, Girl Genius.* New York: Arthur Levine Books, 2003.

———. *Stanford Wong Flunks Big-Time.* New York: Arthur A. Levine Books, 2005.

Zimmerman, Bill. *100 Things Guys Need to Know.* Minneapolis, MN: Free Spirit Publishing, 2005.

Conclusion

With younger kids, the risks are even greater. MySpace is supposedly restricted to users 14 and over. But there is nothing to prevent a younger child with an e-mail address from lying about his or her age and signing up as a member.—(Hewitt, Bill. "MySpace Nation: The Controversy." *People* 65, no. 22 (2006): 113.)

Times are changing. Technology is constantly improving and altering how we live our lives. In an era when online social networking is becoming more prominent, young teens and 'tweens need access to excellent library services that will help them make informed decisions.

As a librarian, you are in a unique role because you can assist with the molding of 'tweens and young teens as they grow into adulthood—you can do this through library programs, services, and collections. Those in the early stage of adolescence, as are 'tweens and young teens, typically need positive adult interaction, and they may seek this type of guidance from you.

'Tweens are neither children nor teenagers, and younger teens typically yearn to be older. Since it is highly likely that the fountain of youth will never be discovered, and that children will eventually become adults, librarians will always need to be prepared for serving an age group that is caught in the middle. 'Tweens and young teens are typically experiencing major changes, and, whether those changes are positive or negative, it is a traumatic time of their lives. Caring librarians who are familiar with the early stage of adolescence and the special circumstances related to this age group can help ease the burden. Hopefully this book has given you some insights, ideas, and support in this important task.

Index

ABOUT THE CONTRIBUTORS

Brenda Hager is the School Library Media Specialist at Dr. James Craik Elementary School in Charles County, Maryland, and previously served as the Youth Services Librarian at the Charlotte Hall Public Library in St. Mary's County, Maryland. She has been a YALSA SUS Trainer since 2001. She is a member of the Maryland Library Association, Maryland Educational Media Association, Association of Library Services to Children, American Association of School Librarians, and the Young Adult Library Services Association.

Robyn Lupa is the Head of Children's Services at the Arvada library of the Jefferson County Public Library in Colorado. She also worked for the Queens Borough Public Library as a young adult librarian. She served on YALSA's Selected DVDs and Videos for Young Adults Committee and the Teen Web Site Advisory Committee. She also served on SRRT's Gay, Lesbian, Bisexual & Transgendered Book Award Committee and ALSC's Preschool Services and Parent Education Committee.

Kristine Mahood is the Young Adult Librarian for the Timberland Regional Library, comprising twenty-seven libraries in five counties in southwest Washington state, where she performs booktalks for teens. She is the author of *A Passion for Print: Promoting Reading and Books to Teens* (Libraries Unlimited, 2006) and the co-author of "The Inner Game of Booktalking," published in the June 2001 issue of *Voice of Youth Advocates*.

James M. Rosinia is the Youth Services Coordinator for the State Library of North Carolina and the co-author of the first edition of *Bare Bones: Young Adult Services, Tips for Public Library Generalists* (American Library Association, 1993). Previously he worked at the Center for the Study of Early Adolescence at the University of North Carolina–Chapel Hill.

Deborah Taylor joined the Enoch Pratt Free Library in Baltimore, Maryland, as a young adult librarian in 1974, and in September 1980 was appointed Young Adult Services Specialist. She is Coordinator of School and Student Services for the Enoch Pratt Free Library. She was a member of the 2006 Best Books for Young Adults Committee, the 2004 Michael Printz Award Committee, the 2002 Newbery Award Committee, and Chair of the 2000 Coretta Scott King Award Jury. She served as YALSA President from 1996–1997. She is an adjunct professor at the University of Maryland, College of Information Studies. As a YALSA Serving the Underserved (SUS) Trainer, she has conducted numerous workshops on youth services in libraries.

ABOUT THE AUTHOR

Sheila B. Anderson has worked for public libraries in North Carolina, Indiana, and Delaware, and is an adjunct instructor for the Department of Library Science at Clarion University of Pennsylvania. She is the editor of *Serving Older Teens* (Libraries Unlimited, 2004) and the author of *Extreme Teens: Library Services to Nontraditional Young Adults* (Libraries Unlimited, 2005). In 2004 she was appointed to the ALA Children's Book Council (CBC) Joint Committee; and she was elected as an ALA Councilor-at-Large in 2003. She has served on the YALSA Board of Directors, the Selected DVDs and Videos for Young Adults Committee, and the Best of the Best Books for Young Adults Preconference Committee. In addition, she is a YALSA Serving the Underserved (SUS) Trainer, a recipient of the Frances Henne/YALSA/VOYA Research Grant, and a winner of the Baker & Taylor/YALSA Conference Grant. She maintains a Web site at www.sheilabanderson.com